Dd

Ee

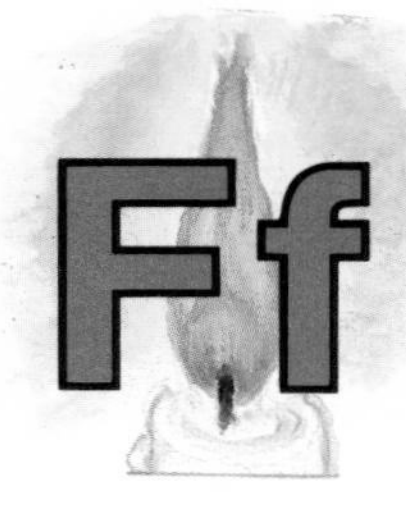
Ff

Kk

Ll

Mm

Qq

Rr

Ss

Tt

Xx

Yy

Zz

ISBN 0 86112 424 3

Published by Brimax Books, Newmarket, England 1987
Second printing 1988.
Printed in Hong Kong

JUNIOR ILLUSTRATED DICTIONARY

Compiled by
Plantagenet Somerset Fry

Illustrated by
Bob Bampton
Norman Barber
Wendy Corbett
John Francis
Tony Gibbons
Bob Hersey
Alan Male
Jane Pickering
Sebastian Quigley
John Rignall
Chris Rothero

Edited by
Trevor Weston

BRIMAX BOOKS · NEWMARKET · ENGLAND

Introduction

What is a dictionary? It is a book that contains a long list of words in alphabetical order and gives their meanings. It also shows how to spell them. Understanding words helps readers to use and write words correctly and to explain themselves quickly and clearly in conversation with others.

On every page in this dictionary there are sentences to show you how many of the words are used, and in the sentences these words appear in **bold** print. Many words have more than one meaning and these are numbered **1, 2, 3** etc.

The book has over 2000 words and 900 illustrations. There are also special pages of picture collectives. These are full pages illustrating objects and people within a particular group – such as animals, birds, costume, dinosaurs, machines, sports and transport.

aardvark an animal with large ears and a long nose. **Aardvarks** feed on ants.

abroad being in or going to another country. We often go **abroad** for our holidays.

accident something unpleasant that happens by mistake.

accordion a musical instrument with bellows and keys. You make music by squeezing the bellows in and out and pressing the keys.

ache a pain that goes on and on, like a head**ache** or tooth**ache**.

acorn the seed of an oak tree.

acrobat a person who does balancing and tumbling tricks. You can see **acrobats** at the circus.

act to take a part in a play or a film.

adder a small, poisonous snake.

address your **address** tells people where you live.

admiral the commander of a large fleet of warships.

adventure something exciting, and sometimes dangerous, that happens.

advertisement words or pictures telling people to buy something.

aeroplane a machine with wings and one or more engines that flies in the air.
(See *transport* – page 141)

afraid scared. You are **afraid** when you believe that someone or something is going to hurt you.

afternoon the time between midday and the evening.

age the number of years that someone or something has lived.

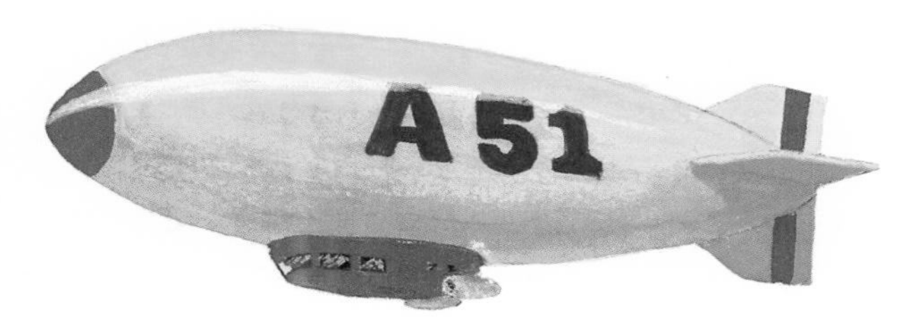

airship a flying machine which is lighter than air. It has an engine and is filled with gas.

alarm **1** a warning sound, like a burglar **alarm**.
2 to frighten. Jane was **alarmed** by the knock at her door in the middle of the night.

album a blank book to put stamps, postcards or photos in.

alive living or full of life.

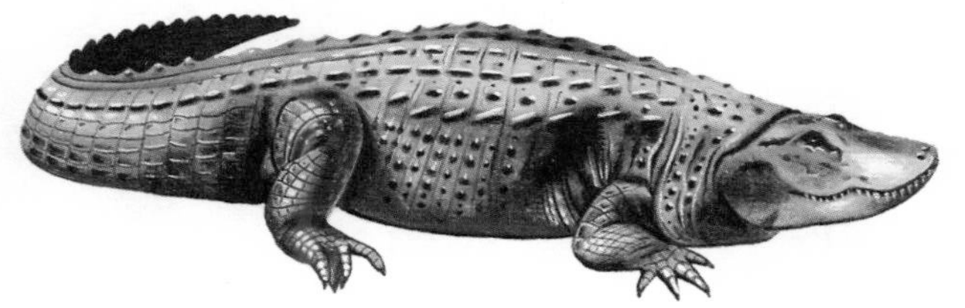

alligator a large reptile like a crocodile with short legs and sharp teeth.

allow to let somebody do something. Jill **allows** her brother to use her bicycle.

alphabet all the letters from a to z you use to make words.

altar a sacred stone table in church where the priest stands.

alter to change or make different. Sara's coat was **altered** to fit her sister.

ambulance a car or small bus for taking people who are sick or injured to hospital.

amount how much or how many you have.

amuse to entertain someone by making them smile or laugh.

anchor a heavy metal hook on a long chain. It is dropped into the sea to keep a ship from moving.

ancient very old or in times of long ago.

angel a messenger from God. The **angel** of the Lord came down.

angry feeling very annoyed. I will be **angry** if you come into the house with mud on your shoes.

animal anything which lives, breathes and can move. (See page 11)

ankle the joint between your foot and the bottom of your leg.

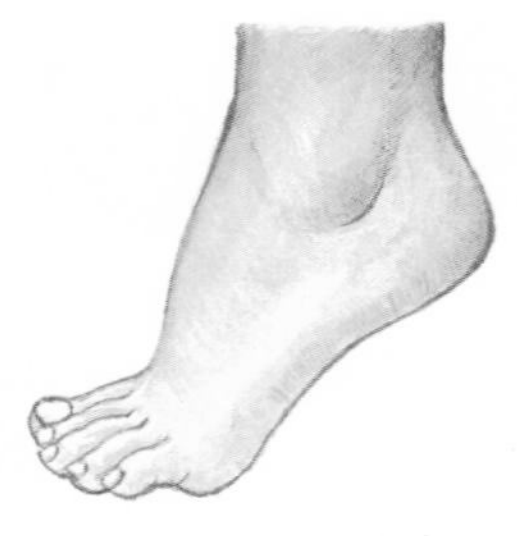

annual 1 every year. Christmas is an **annual** event.
2 a book that comes out once a year.

anorak a jacket with a hood to keep out wind and rain.

answer what you reply to a written or spoken question.

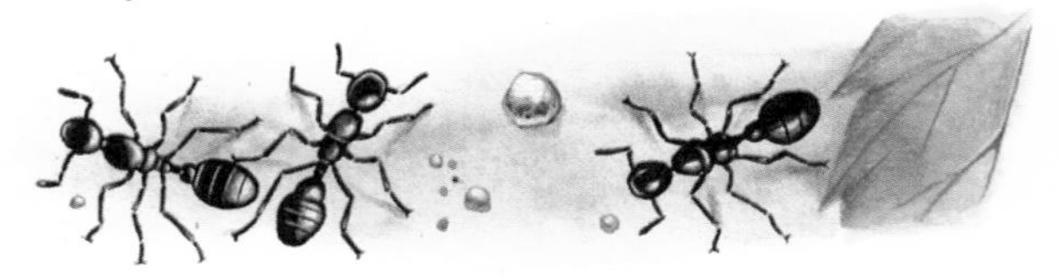

ant a tiny insect which lives and works in groups of thousands.

anteater a wild animal with a long sticky tongue which feeds on ants.

antelope an animal like a deer, with long curved horns.

apartment a large room, or group of rooms, on one floor of a building. Some people live in **apartments**.

ape a wild animal like a monkey. **Apes** have long arms and no tail.

apologise to say you are sorry. Mary **apologised** to her mother for spilling lemonade on the carpet.

appendix a short tube inside your body. Sometimes it swells up and needs to be taken out in the hospital.

animals
dog
monkey
cat
bat
porcupine
horse
rabbit
tortoise
mouse
lion
buffalo
cow

Aa

apple a round hard fruit with a red, yellow or green skin.

apricot a juicy fruit, like a small peach, with a big stone inside.

apron a piece of cloth you tie around your waist to keep your clothes clean when cooking or washing dishes.

aquarium a tank with glass sides filled with water. You keep fish and water animals in an **aquarium**.

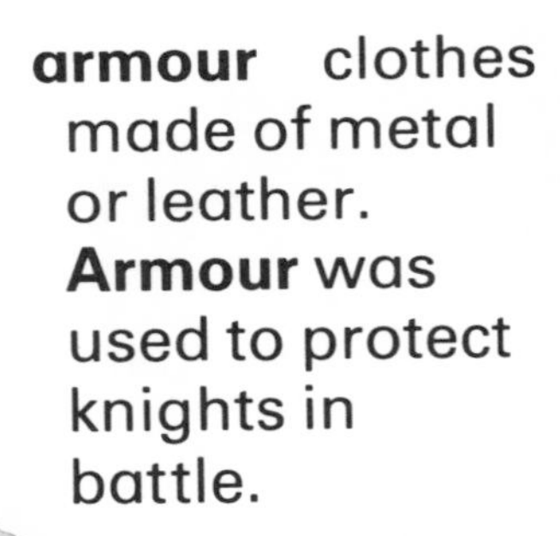

archer someone who shoots arrows from a curved stick of wood called a bow.

argue to disagree in words. John and Mary **argued** about where to have a picnic.

arithmetic counting with numbers, like addition, subtraction, multiplication and division.

ark the huge boat Noah built to save the animals from the Flood.

arm the part of your body between your shoulder and your hand.

armchair a chair with sides to rest your arms on.

armour clothes made of metal or leather. **Armour** was used to protect knights in battle.

army a great number of soldiers.

arrive to reach the place you are travelling to. Tom **arrived** at the bus stop outside the school.

arrow a long thin stick with a sharp point. You shoot an **arrow** from a bow.

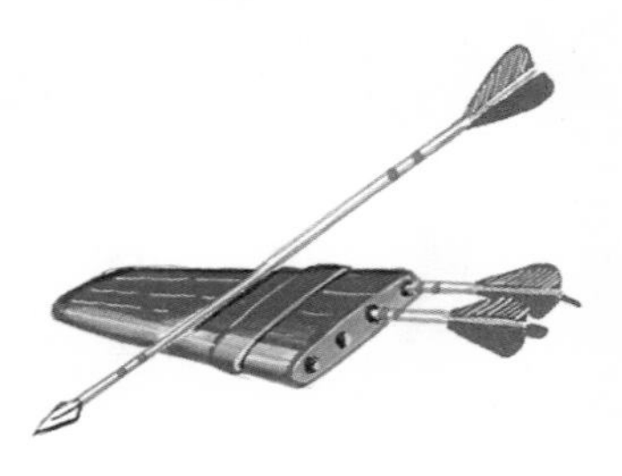

artist someone who paints or draws pictures.

ash **1** the powder that remains when something is burned.
2 a type of tree.

asleep sleeping, not awake.

astronaut someone who travels through space in a spaceship.

athlete somebody who is good at games like running, jumping and throwing.

atlas a book containing maps of parts of the world.

audience a group of people who have come to hear or to watch something.

aunt a sister of your father or mother, or the wife of your uncle.

autograph someone's name written in their own handwriting. Suzy collects **autographs** of famous pop stars.

autumn the season of the year between summer and winter.

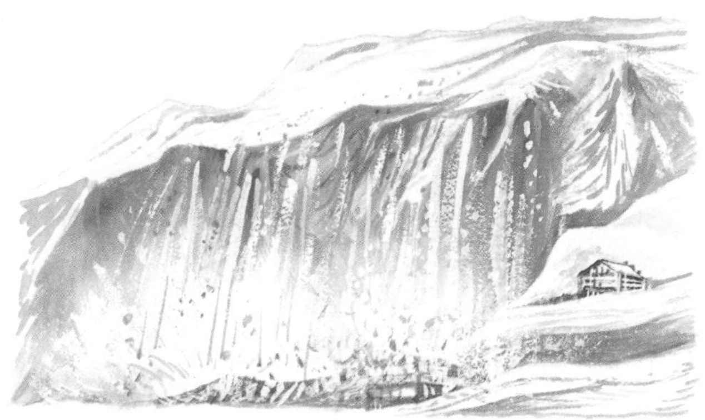

avalanche a large mass of snow, ice and rocks which breaks away from a mountainside and crashes downwards.

awake not asleep.

awful very bad. Sandy says he has an **awful** toothache.

axe a chopping tool with a long handle. An **axe** is used for chopping wood.

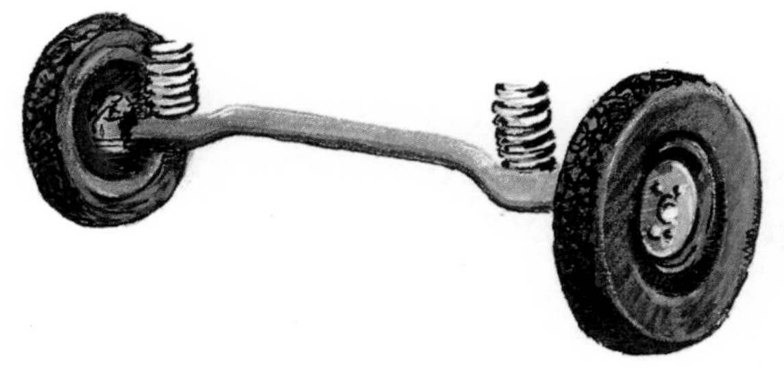

axle an iron rod with a wheel at each end which turns.

baby buggy a chair on wheels that a baby is moved around in outdoors.

bacon meat from part of a pig. Sometimes I have **bacon** and eggs for breakfast.

badge something you pin or sew to your clothes for decoration.

bag a container made of cloth, paper or plastic that you carry things in.

baker someone who bakes and sells bread and cakes.

bald having little or no hair. My grandfather was **bald** so he wore a hat to keep his head warm.

ballet a dance that tells a story using mime and music.

balloon **1** a little bag of thin rubber. When you blow up a **balloon** it floats in the air.
2 a form of transport that uses hot air to make the **balloon** float across the sky. (See *transport* – page 141)

banana a long thin fruit with a yellow skin.

band **1** a group of people who play music for entertainment.
2 a strip of leather, rubber or metal that holds things together. The cards were held together with a rubber **band**.

bandage a piece of cloth you use to tie round a cut or sore.

bang a very sudden loud noise, like a door slamming.

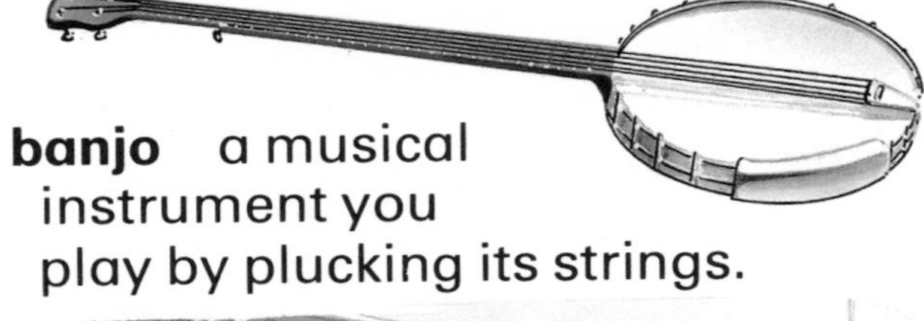

banjo a musical instrument you play by plucking its strings.

bank **1** a building where you leave your money to be looked after.
2 the ground along the side of a river.

bar 1 a long piece of metal or wood.
2 the part of a hotel or café where you order drinks.

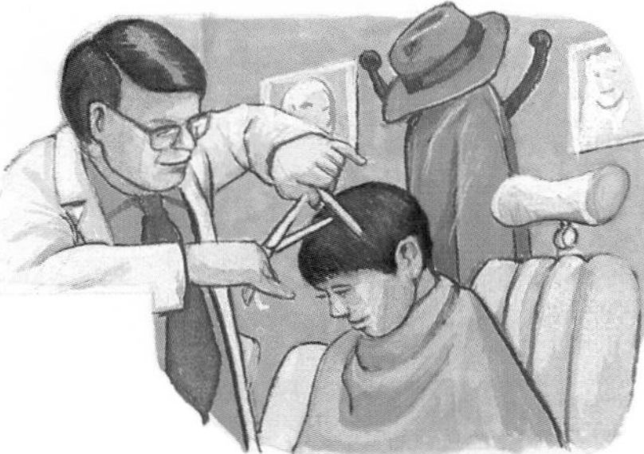

barber someone who cuts men's and boys' hair.

bare 1 wearing no clothes.
2 empty. When she got there, the cupboard was **bare**.

bargain something you buy or sell cheaply.

barge a flat-bottomed boat for carrying people or goods on rivers or canals.

bark 1 the covering on a tree trunk.
2 the loud noise made by dogs.

barley a grain crop used for making some drinks and food.

barn a building used by a farmer to store crops or as a house for his animals.

barrel a round wooden container held together with iron bands.

baseball a game played with bat and ball between two teams of nine players. The batting side tries to score by hitting the ball and then running round a diamond-shaped field. (See *sports* – page 128)

basement the bottom rooms of a house below the ground.

basket a bag made of plastic, wire or wooden strips that you carry things in.

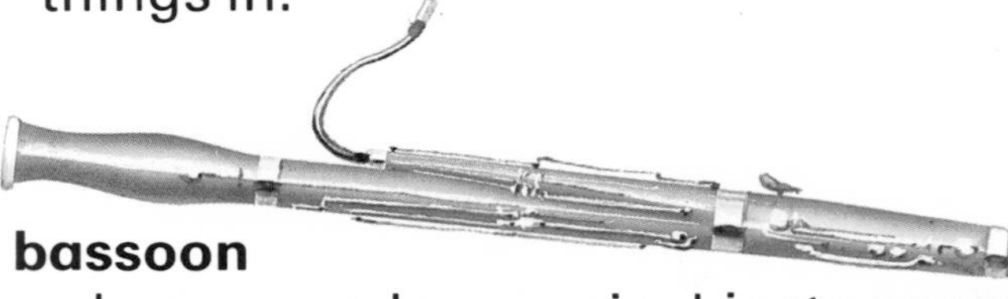

bassoon a large wooden musical instrument.

bat 1 a piece of wood specially made for hitting balls in some games.
2 a small flying animal that looks like a mouse with wings. (See *animals* – page 11)

bath a big tub which you fill with water and sit in to wash yourself all over.

bathroom the small room in your house where the bath is.

batsman the person who holds the bat in a game like cricket.

battering ram a long heavy pole which attackers used in past times to break down a castle door or wall.

battery a container that stores electricity. My radio runs on **batteries**.

battle a fight between armies, ships or aeroplanes in a war.

bay part of the sea where it makes a curve in the coastline.

bayonet a sharp blade you can fix to the end of a rifle.

beach a place covered in sand or pebbles where the land meets the sea.

beacon a light at sea or on land that is lit to warn of danger.

beak the hard part around a bird's mouth.

bean a vegetable you cook and eat. One kind of **bean** is cooked in tomato sauce to make baked **beans**.

bear 1 a large furry wild animal.
2 to carry or hold up. This shelf will not **bear** the weight of all these books.

beard the hair on a man's chin or cheeks.

beautiful very pretty, very lovely. Ann's sister has become a **beautiful** woman.

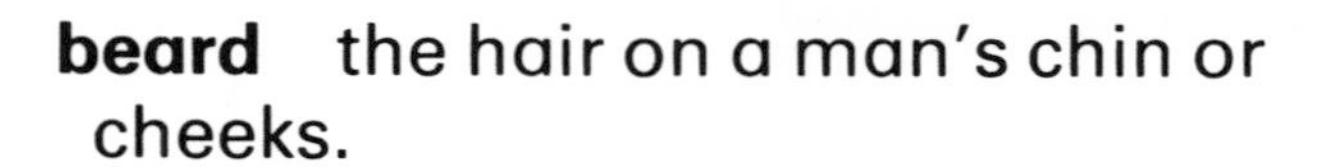

beaver a small furry animal with strong, sharp, front teeth. **Beavers** chew through trees to build their homes in rivers and streams.

bedroom the room where you go to sleep every night.

Bb

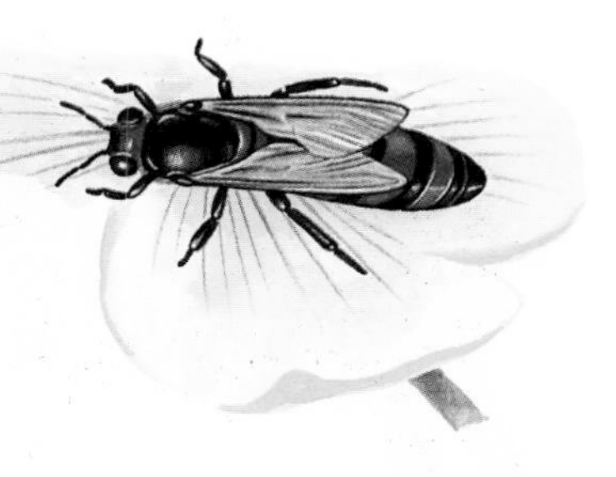

bee a small flying insect that makes honey.

beech a tree with dark green shiny leaves that grows very tall.

beer a drink made from hops and malt.

beetle an insect with six legs and a hard skin.

beg to ask very humbly for something.

begin to start. Let's **begin** reading this book tonight.

believe to feel sure that something is true. I **believe** in Santa Claus.

bell a hollow metal cup that makes a ringing sound when you hit it.

bellows an instrument used for blowing air into a fire to make it burn.

belt a band of cloth, leather or plastic you wear around your waist. You can fasten a **belt** with a buckle.

bench **1** a long wooden seat.
2 a wooden table used for work like carpentry.

bend **1** a curve. There is a sharp **bend** in the road beyond the church.
2 to make something curve. A strong man can **bend** an iron bar.

beret (sounds like berray) a round flat hat made of soft material.

berry a small juicy fruit with lots of seeds, like a rasp**berry** or a straw**berry**.

between in the middle of two things. The road runs **between** the river and the railway track.

Bible the book about the history of the Jews and the life of Jesus Christ.

bicycle a two-wheeled vehicle that you ride.

bind to tie things together.

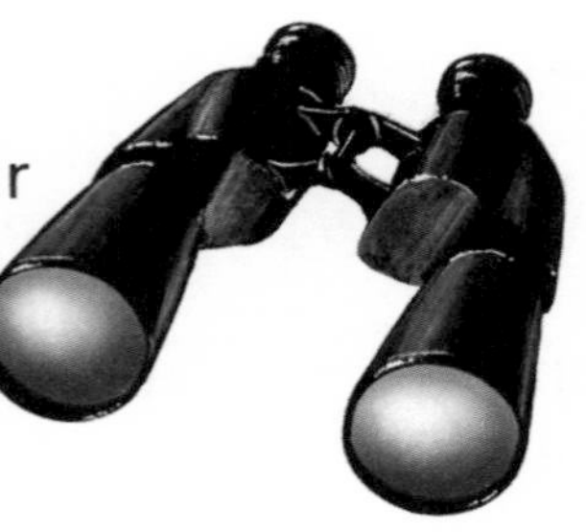

binoculars a pair of eyeglasses that make distant objects seem larger.

bird a feathered animal with two legs and two wings. (See page 19)

birdcage a small container made of wire in which pet birds are kept.

birthday the day someone was born.

bishop a priest who is in charge of several churches over a large area.

bison a wild North American animal like a buffalo.

bite **1** to cut into something using your teeth.
2 an injury caused when an animal **bites** you.

bitter not sweet. Lemon juice without sugar tastes **bitter**.

blackbird a bird with black feathers and a yellow beak.

blackboard a piece of wood painted black that you write on with white or coloured chalk.

blacksmith a craftsman who makes or mends things of iron or steel.

birds
goose
pigeon
thrush
wren
raven
sparrow
magpie
dove
crane
canary
penguin
swan

blade 1 the sharp cutting edge of a knife.
2 a single leaf of grass.

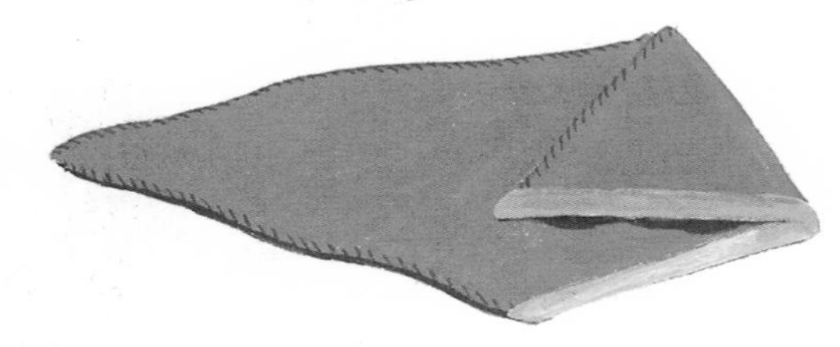

blanket a warm woollen cover you put over the top sheet of your bed.

blaze 1 a white marking on the front of an animal's face.
2 to burn fiercely. The dry straw on the burning roof **blazed** all night.

blazer a short jacket that some children wear as part of a school uniform.

blind 1 not able to see.
2 a type of screen that can be pulled down or across a window.

blindfold to cover someone's eyes with a cloth so they cannot see.

blink to open and shut your eyes very quickly.

blister a watery swelling on your skin which can be painful.

blizzard a snowstorm driven by very strong winds.

block 1 a big piece of wood or stone. He built the wall using large stone **blocks**.
2 to be in the way. The road was **blocked** by heavy snow.

blood the red liquid running through your body.

blotting paper soft thick paper which you use to dry ink marks on a sheet of paper.

blouse a buttoned shirt worn by women and girls.

blow 1 to breathe air quickly out of your mouth.
2 a sudden hit with your hand or a weapon.

board 1 a long flat piece of wood such as a floor**board**.
2 to get on to a ship or train or aeroplane.

boat something that floats on water carrying people or goods.

body the whole of a person or animal.

bodyguard a person who guards someone important.

boil 1 to heat water so hot that it bubbles. Did you **boil** the water to make the coffee?
2 a very painful spot or swelling on the body.

bolt 1 a thick metal pin like a screw that can hold things together.
2 a sliding metal fastener for a door.

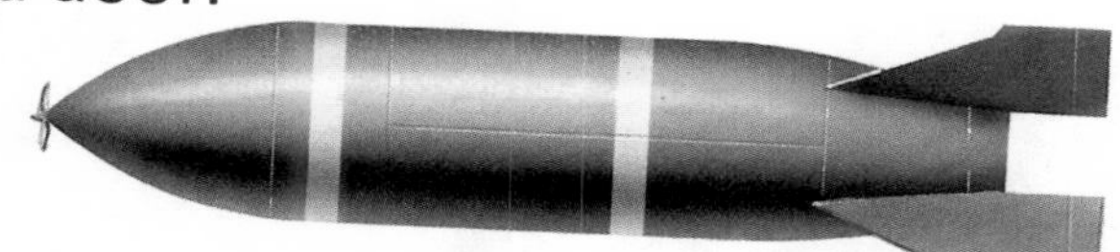

bomb a hollow metal container filled with an explosive that blows up and can cause a lot of damage.

bone the hard parts inside the body. All your **bones** together make up your skeleton.

bonfire a small fire outdoors.

book sheets of printed paper fastened together inside a cover.

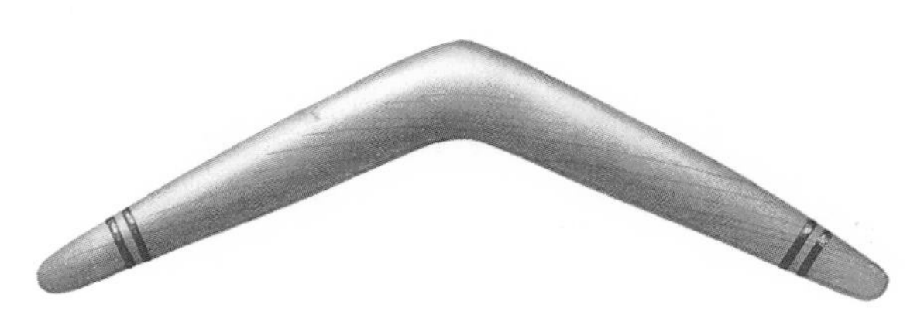

boomerang a curved wooden stick used in Australia. When you throw a **boomerang** in the air it comes back to you.

boot a kind of shoe made of leather or rubber, that covers your foot and part of your leg.

border 1 the line between two countries. We crossed the Mexican **border**.
2 the edge of something like a page or a garden.

borrow to use something you will give back to its owner when you have finished with it.

both two together; the two of them. **Both** my sisters are older than me.

bother to worry or annoy someone.

bottle a container made of glass or plastic for holding water or other liquids.

bottom **1** the lowest part; the underneath. My friend dropped a stone to the **bottom** of the pond.
2 the part of your body you sit on.

boulder a very large rock.

bounce to make something jump up again after hitting the ground. He **bounced** the ball along the path.

boundary a line that marks a division between two pieces of land.

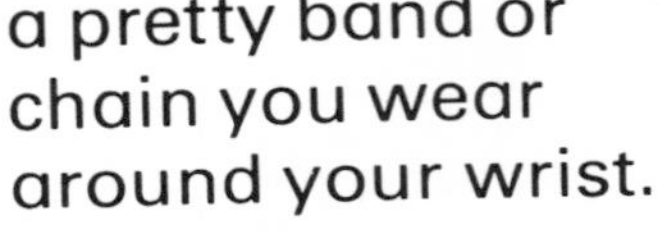

bow (rhymes with low) **1** a knot you tie in a piece of string or ribbon.
2 a curved stick archers use to shoot arrows.
3 a stick with hairs stretched from one end to the other used to play a violin or cello.
4 (rhymes with cow) to bend forward and lower your head as a mark of respect.

bowl a deep round dish.

box a container of wood, metal or cardboard that has straight sides and a lid.

boxer someone who fights for sport. **Boxers** wear gloves and fight in boxing rings.

bracelet a pretty band or chain you wear around your wrist.

brain the part of your body inside your skull that makes every other part of your body work.

brake the part of a machine or a vehicle that makes the wheels slow down or stop.

branch an arm of a tree.

brave ready to face danger. She was **brave** enough to chase the burglar out of the house.

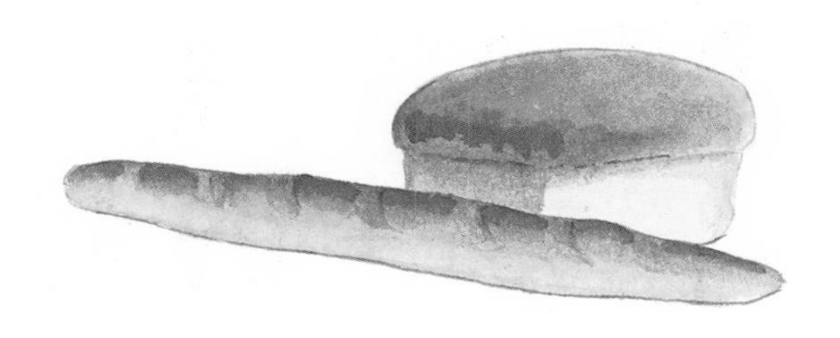

bread a food made by baking flour, water and yeast in an oven.

break 1 to smash or split into pieces.
2 a rest. We will have a **break** at the end of the lesson.

breakfast the first meal of the day.

breathe to take air into your lungs and let it out again.

breeze a light, gentle wind.

brick a block of clay baked to make it hard. **Bricks** are used in building work.

bride a woman on her wedding day.

bridge a raised piece of road or path built over a road, river or railway so that people or traffic can go across.

bright 1 giving out a lot of light.
2 clever, quick to learn. Susan is one of the **brightest** girls in her class.

brim 1 the edge of a cup or bowl.
2 the flat part of a hat that sticks out all around.

bring to fetch or carry. **Bring** in a packed lunch tomorrow.

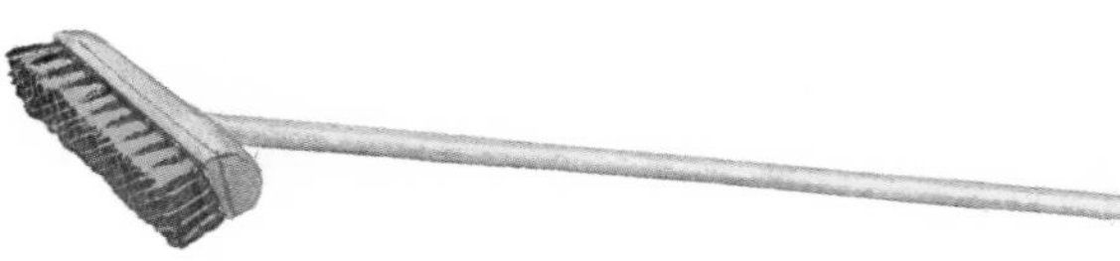

broom a brush on a long handle used for sweeping.

brother a boy or man who has the same mother and father as the other children in a family.

bruise a mark under your skin you get after you have been injured by a sharp blow.

brush a tool with short stiff hairs on a handle. **Brushes** can be used for painting or sweeping or for tidying your hair.

bubble a shiny ball with air inside made with soap and water.

bucket a metal or plastic container with a handle. **Buckets** are often used for carrying water.

buckle a fastener on a belt or a shoe. Mary has a gold **buckle** on her belt.

bud a young flower or leaf that is tightly rolled up before it is ready to open.

buffalo a wild animal like an ox that lives in Africa and North America. (See *animals* – page 11)

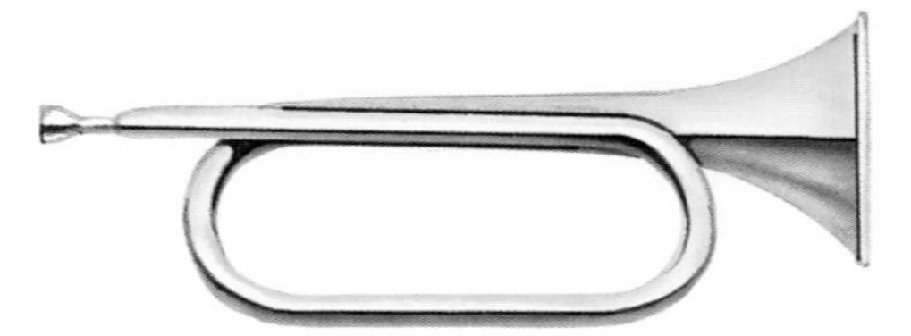

bugle a musical instrument like a small trumpet usually played at army parades.

building something that is built. Houses, schools and office blocks are **buildings**.

bulb **1** the onion-shaped root of some flowers.
2 the glass part of an electric light that shines.

bull the name for the male of some large animals. Male cattle are **bulls**.

bulldozer a large vehicle with a scoop at the front that moves earth and rubble.

bullet a piece of lead you shoot from a pistol or rifle.

bundle a collection of things tied up together. We bought a **bundle** of sticks to make an open fire.

bungalow a house that has all its rooms on the ground floor.

buoy a floating marker anchored in the sea to guide ships.

burglar someone who breaks into buildings to steal things.

burn **1** to be on fire.
2 to set fire to something.
3 an injury caused by fire.

burrow a hole in the ground that some wild animals dig to make homes for themselves.

burst to split open suddenly; to explode. The balloon **burst** when I sat on it.

bury to put something into a hole in the ground and then cover it up.

bus a very large vehicle that can carry a lot of people who pay for their ride.

bus stop a place in the street where people get on or off buses.

bush a plant with lots of branches growing near the ground.

business **1** someone's work.
2 a shop, factory or firm.

busy having a lot to do.

butcher someone who cuts up meat and sells it.

butter a soft yellow food made from cream.

buttercup a small yellow wild flower.

butterfly an insect with coloured wings that flies around in hot weather.

button a small round fastening on many clothes.

buy to get something by handing over money for it.

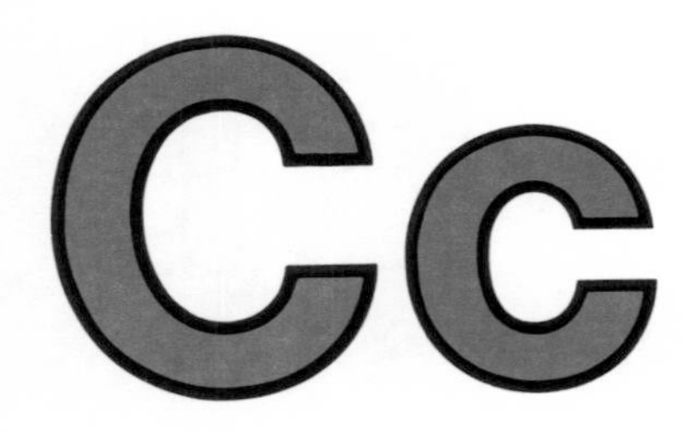

cabbage a green vegetable with thick leaves you can cook and eat.

café a place where you can get something to eat and drink.

cage a box or room with bars where animals and birds can be kept. You will often find **cages** at the zoo.

cake a sweet food made with flour, butter, eggs and sugar and baked in an oven.

calculator a machine for working out sums very quickly.

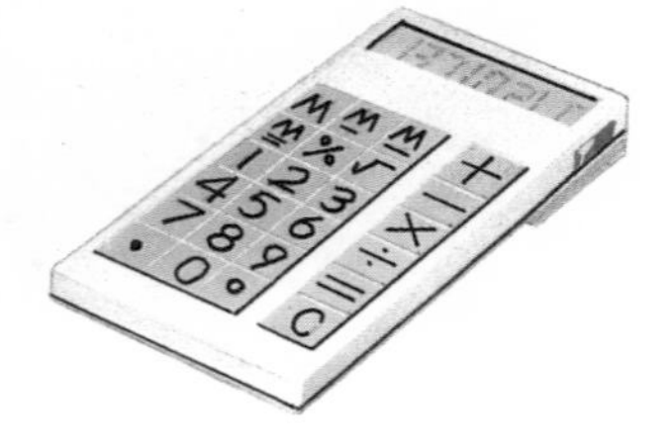

calendar a sheet or sheets of paper showing all the days and months of the year.

calf **1** a young bull or cow.
2 the back part of your leg below the knee.

calm still or quiet. It was a **calm** evening with no wind.

camel a large animal with one or two humps on its back that lives in the desert.

camera a kind of box you put film in to take photographs.

camp **1** to live in a tent. We sometimes go **camping** for our holidays.
2 a collection of tents and caravans where people live.

canal a kind of river that is made by people for boats and barges to use.

canary a small yellow bird you can keep as a pet. (See *birds* – page 19)

candle a stick of wax with string through the centre which you burn to make a light.

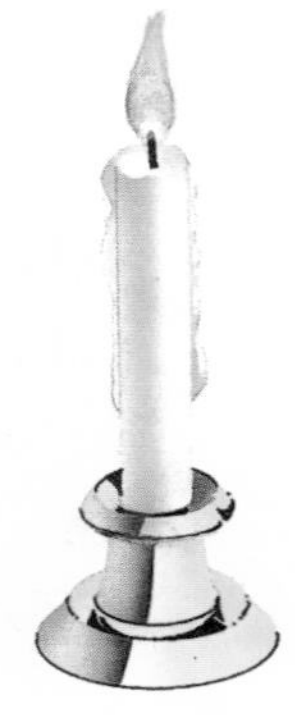

cannon a huge gun that can fire heavy iron balls.

canoe a small narrow boat that you paddle along the water.

capital 1 the main city of a country. Washington D. C. is the **capital** of the United States of America.
2 a big letter of the alphabet. A, B and C are **capital** letters.

captain 1 the leader of a team.
2 an officer in the navy or army.

capture to take prisoner in battle.

car a machine on four wheels that travels on roads.
(See *transport*—page 141)

caravan a small house on wheels that can be pulled along by a car.

card 1 one of a set of playing pieces made of **card** with numbers and pictures on. There are lots of different games you can play with **cards**.
2 stiff paper.
3 a piece of **card** with a picture and a message on. You send a **card** to mark a special day.

careful taking care. Be **careful** when you cross the road.

cargo the goods a ship or an aircraft carries.

carnival a party or parade in the open air. People often wear fancy dress at **carnivals.**

carol a religious song we sing at Christmas time.

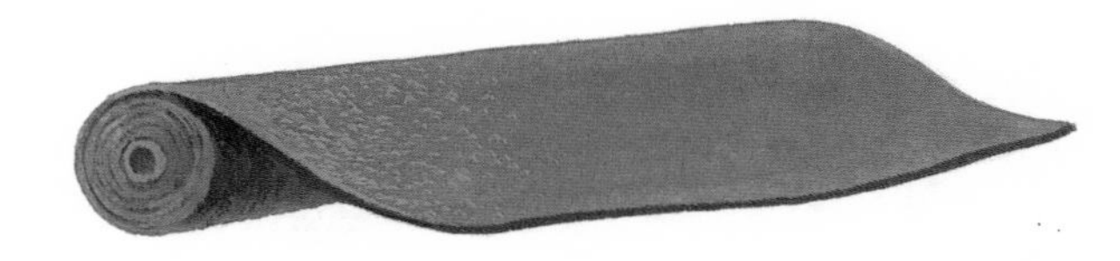

carpet a heavy material that covers the floor.

carriage 1 a horse-drawn cart that people can travel in.
2 one of the sections of a train where passengers sit.

carrot a long orange vegetable which grows under the ground.

carry to pick something up and take it away.

Cc

cart an open-topped wooden truck usually pulled by a horse or donkey.

carve **1** to cut meat into slices.
2 to cut wood or stone into special shapes.

case a box or chest for carrying or holding things.

cassette a small plastic case with a reel of recording tape inside.

castle a large strong building with thick stone walls. **Castles** were built to protect the people inside from attackers.

cat a furry animal you can keep as a pet. (See *animals* – page 11)

catapult
a large machine used long ago that threw big stones to knock down walls.

catch **1** to get hold of something. Sometimes my brother **catches** fish in the river.
2 a kind of lock on a door or window.

caterpillar
a small creeping creature that turns into a butterfly or a moth.

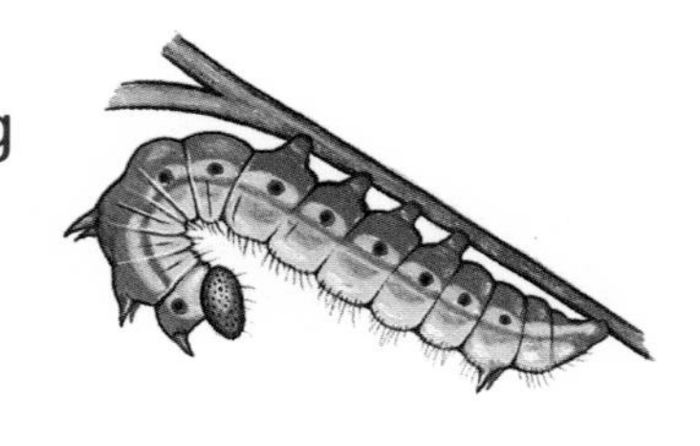

cathedral a huge church in a city.

cattle a group of cows, bulls and calves.

cauldron
a large hanging pot used for cooking.

cauliflower a vegetable that has a hard white part in the middle you can eat.

cave a large hole in the side of a hill or under ground. Many years ago people lived in **caves**.

ceiling the top of a room.

celery a vegetable which has long white stems you can eat raw or cooked.

cello (sounds like chello) a large stringed instrument you play with a bow.

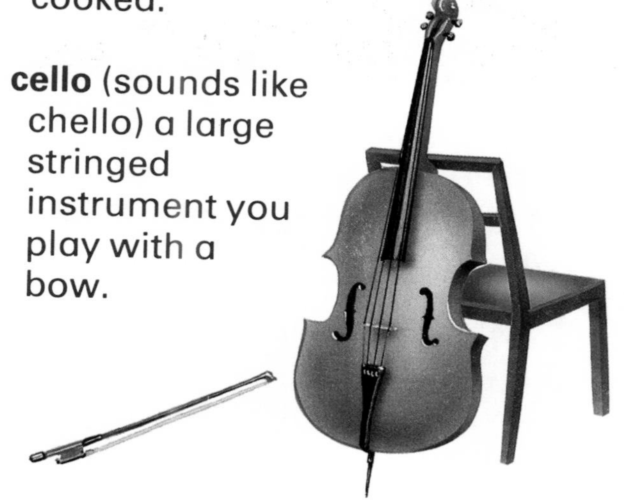

cement mixer a machine that mixes a kind of clay used in building work.
(See *machines* – page 78)

cent a coin of very small value. There are 100 **cents** in a dollar.

centimetre a short measurement of length. There are 100 **centimetres** in one metre.

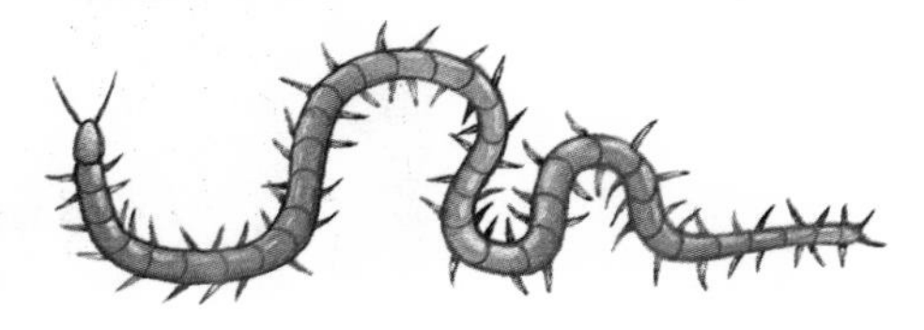

centipede a small creeping creature that has many legs.

centre **1** the middle part or middle point of something.
2 a place for important activities, like the **centre** of town.

century one hundred years.

certain sure; knowing something is true. Jim was **certain** he had posted the letter.

certificate a piece of paper that is given to a person who has done something special. Debbie was given a **certificate** for swimming 100 metres.

chain a line of metal rings joined together.

chair a seat for one person.

chalk soft white or coloured stone used for writing on a blackboard.

champion the winner of a contest.

change **1** the money you get back if you pay too much for something.
2 to put something in place of something else.
3 to put on different clothes.

Cc

chapter a part of a reading book. The last book I read had ten **chapters**.

chariot a two-wheeled cart pulled by horses. Long ago, Romans used **chariots** for racing and fighting.

chase to run after. Our dog **chases** the neighbour's cat.

cheap not costing very much. The meal at the café was **cheap**.

cheerful happy.

cheese a food made from milk which you can eat raw or cooked.

cheetah a large wild cat that can run very fast.

cherry a small round red fruit with a stone in the middle.

chess a game for two people played on a board of black and white squares using pieces called **chess**men.

chest **1** the upper front part of your body.
2 a large strong box used for storing things.

chicken a young hen.

chicken pox an illness that gives you spots on your skin that itch.

chief
1 the leader. Geronimo was **chief** of an American Indian tribe.
2 the most important.

child a boy or girl older than a baby but not grown up.

chimney an opening that runs above a fireplace through the wall to the roof. Smoke and sparks from a fire come out through the **chimney**.

Cc

chimpanzee an ape that is smaller than a gorilla. **Chimpanzees** can do clever tricks.

chin the part of your face under your mouth.

chip a long thin piece of fried potato.

chocolate a brown sweet made from cocoa.

choir (sounds like quire) a group of people who sing together. There is often a **choir** in church.

choose to pick out one thing from several others.

chop **1** a thick slice of meat.
2 to cut something up with an axe or a heavy knife.

Christian someone who follows the teachings of Jesus Christ.

Christmas the birthday of Jesus Christ on December 25th.

church a building where people pray and sing hymns.

cigar tobacco leaves rolled up together for smoking.

cigarette tobacco leaves chopped up and put into a thin paper roll for smoking.

cinema a building where you go to see films.

circle anything shaped like a ring. We stood in a **circle** to play the game.

circus a travelling show of animals, clowns and acrobats doing tricks.

city a very large town.

Cc

clap to hit your hands together to show you enjoyed something.

clarinet a musical instrument that you play by blowing down it and pressing keys.

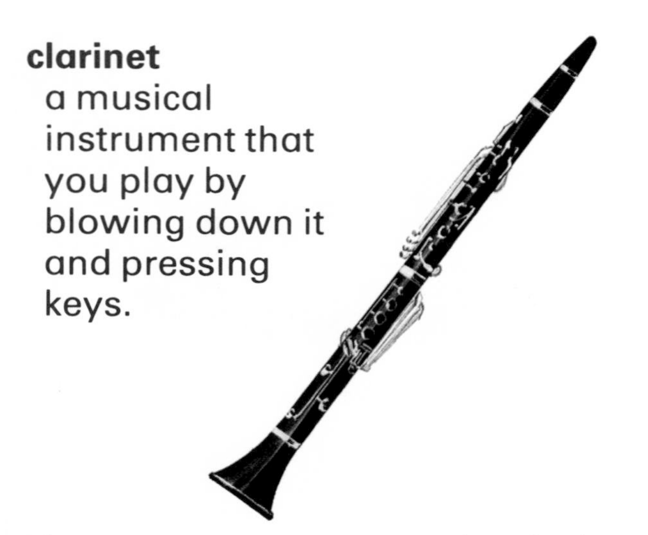

classroom a room at school where we take lessons.

claw the sharp nail on the foot of a bird. Some animals also have **claws**.

clay soft earth that is baked to make pottery or bricks for building houses.

clean without any dirt.

clear **1** to move something away from its place. Will you **clear** your toys off the table, please?
2 simple, easy to understand.
3 bright and sunny. The sky is **clear** and very blue today.

clever able to do things very well.

cliff a steep rock face near the seaside.

climb to move up or down something steep, using hands and feet to hold on.

cloak a loose coat that has no sleeves.

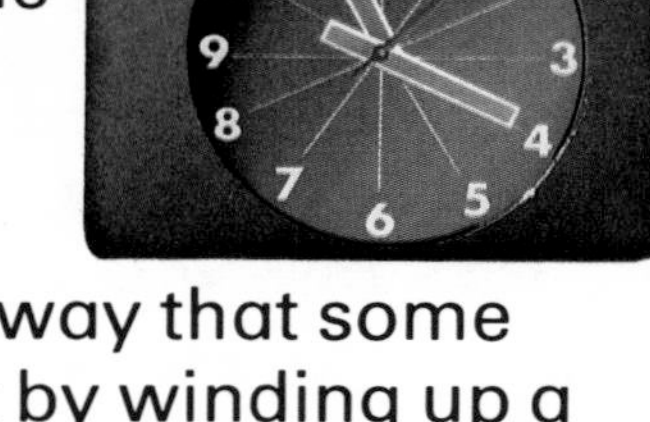

clock a machine that tells you the time.

clockwork the way that some machines work by winding up a spring with a key. My model train has a **clockwork** motor.

closed shut. School is **closed** on Sunday.

cloth **1** material used to make things like clothes, sheets and curtains.
2 a piece of **cloth** used for cleaning or covering something.

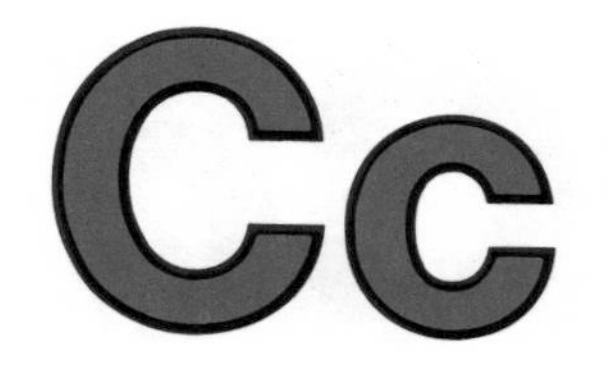

clothes the things you wear during the day.

cloud a white, grey or black mass that floats in the sky. **Clouds** are made from drops of water and bits of dust.

clown a funny man with a painted face you see at the circus.

club 1 a heavy wooden stick.
2 a group of people interested in the same thing who meet together.

clue something that helps to give an answer to a difficult problem like an unsolved mystery.

clumsy always knocking things over or dropping them.

coach 1 a large carriage pulled by horses.
2 a bus with one floor you travel in for long journeys.

coal a hard black rock that miners dig out of the ground. **Coal** is used for burning on fires.

coast land at the edge of the sea. Our neighbours went to the **coast** at the weekend.

cobra a poisonous snake.

cobweb the very fine net a spider makes to trap insects for food.

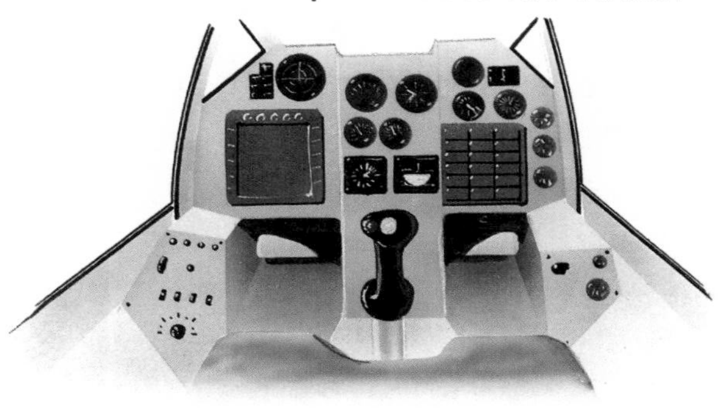

cockpit the seat for a pilot in an aircraft or a driver in a racing car.

coconut a very large hairy nut with white flesh and milk inside.

code a system of signs for secret writing.

coffee a hot drink made from roasted **coffee** beans.

coin a piece of money made of metal.

cold **1** not hot. It is very **cold** when it snows.
2 a mild illness when you have a running nose and sneeze a lot.

collar the part of a coat or shirt that goes around your neck.

collect to gather things together. My brother **collects** stamps.

comb a short strip of plastic or metal with teeth along one edge used for tidying your hair.

combine harvester a huge machine farmers use to cut and thresh their crops.

comfortable pleasant to be in, or to sit on. This armchair is more **comfortable** than the stool.

comic a picture paper for young people.

compass an instrument that shows you where north, south, east and west are.

competition a test or a game which usually has prizes for the winners.

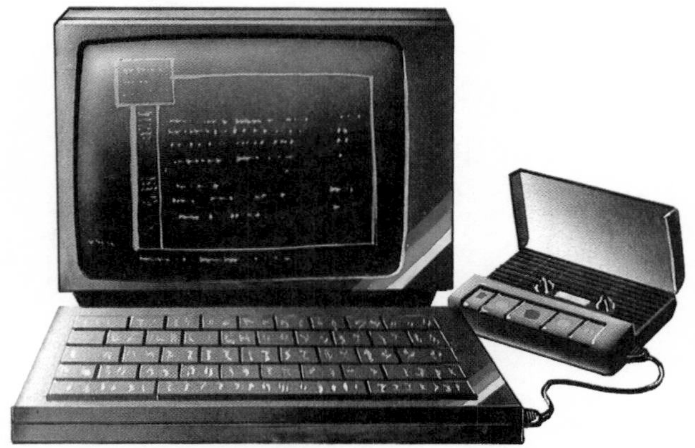

computer a machine with a keyboard and a screen that can do difficult calculations very quickly.

concert a form of entertainment where music is played to an audience.

concrete a mixture of cement, sand and water that sets hard. **Concrete** is used in building work.

conductor **1** someone who directs the players of musical instruments in an orchestra.
2 someone who collects the money you pay when you ride on a bus.

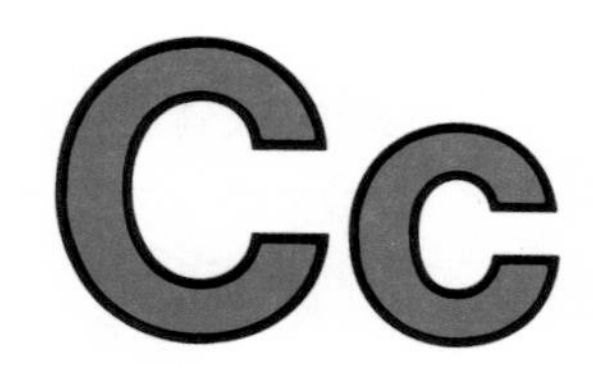

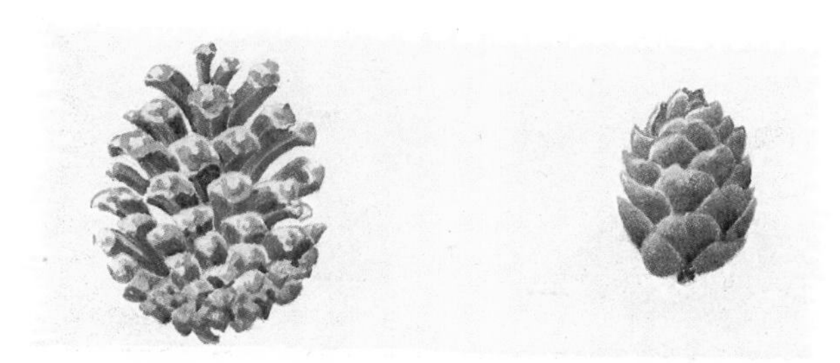

cone **1** the fruit of a fir tree.
2 a shape like a witch's hat, round at the bottom and pointed at the top.
3 the **cone**-shaped biscuit that you eat with ice cream in it.

confetti very small pieces of coloured paper you throw over a bride and bridegroom at their wedding.

cook **1** someone who prepares and heats food for meals.
2 to prepare and heat food before eating it.

copy to do or make something exactly the same as somebody else.

core the hard middle part of some fruits. Apples and pears have **cores**.

cork a stopper for a bottle or jar.

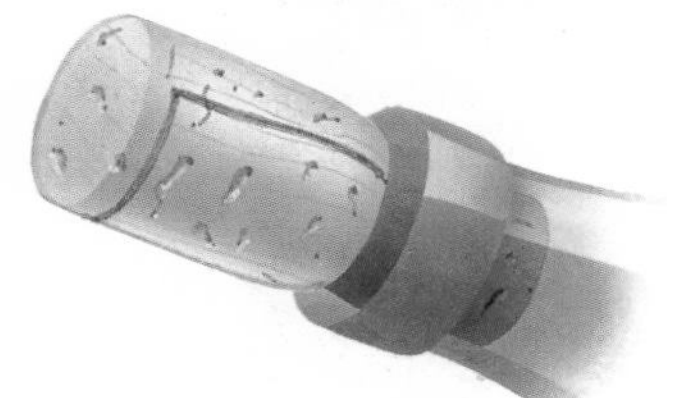

corn the seed of some grain plants like wheat, barley and rye.

corner the place where two walls or two roads meet.

cornet a musical instrument that looks like a small trumpet.

cornflakes a breakfast food made from baked corn and eaten with milk.

cosmonaut the word Russians use for someone who travels in space.

costume **1** the way people dress in different countries. (See page 36)
2 the clothes worn in plays and films about long ago.

cottage a small house in the countryside.

cotton the white fluffy substance that grows on the **cotton** plant. **Cotton** is made into a kind of thread that can be woven into cloth.

cotton wool a soft fluffy material made from cotton. **Cotton wool** is used for cleaning skin and bandaging wounds.

cough a noise you make to clear your throat. Smoke and bad colds make people **cough**.

costumes
Balinese
Indian
Dutch
Saudi-
Arabian
Greek
Nigerian
Japanese
Spanish
Hawaiian
Peruvian
Scottish
Russian

Cc

count to find out how many by saying the numbers in order. My brother can **count** to ten on his fingers.

counter **1** a long table in a shop or a café where you are served.
2 a disc used in some games.

country a large area of land that belongs to a nation of people.

countryside the land that is outside towns and cities.

courage great bravery.

cousin a child of your uncle or your aunt.

cover to place one thing over another, usually to hide or protect it. **Cover** the table with an old cloth before you start painting.

cow the animal that gives milk. (See *animals* – page 11)

cowboy someone who lives on a ranch and looks after cattle. **Cowboys** are usually found in the United States of America.

crab a sea creature with a hard shell on its back. **Crabs** have eight legs and two claws at the front.

cracker **1** a kind of hard flat biscuit.
2 a paper toy that makes a bang when you pull it.

craftsman someone who is very skilled, using his hands to make things.

crane **1** a machine that lifts heavy objects and moves them about. (See *machines* – page 78)
2 a water bird with long legs. (See *birds* – page 19)

crash **1** a car accident.
2 the loud noise of something being broken suddenly.

crawl to move very slowly on your hands and knees.

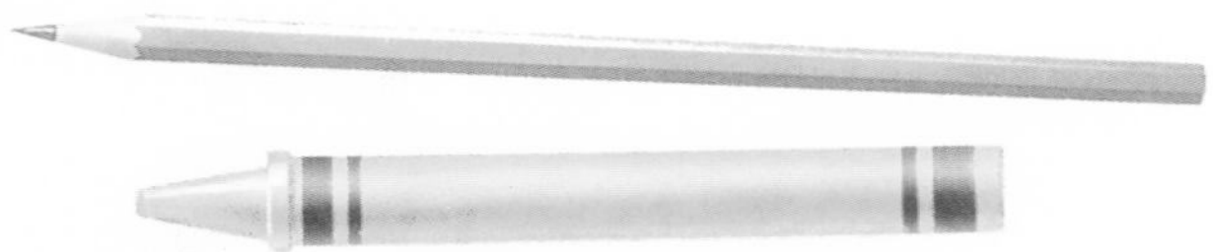

crayon a colouring pencil or a stick of coloured wax.

crazy mad or foolish.

cream the thick liquid on the top of the milk. Sometimes **cream** is beaten to eat with cakes and desserts.

creature any animal.

creep to move along very slowly and very quietly.

crew a group of people working on a ship or an aircraft.

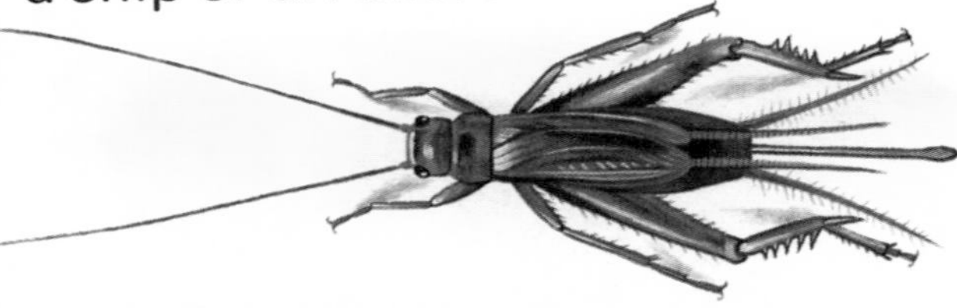

cricket **1** an insect that jumps around and makes a 'click-click' noise.
2 a game for two teams of 11 players who use bats, a ball and two wickets. (See *sports* – page 128)

crime an action that breaks the law.

crisps thin slices of fried potatoes.

crocodile a large and dangerous water animal that lives in hot countries.

cross **1** angry.
2 a mark like + or x.
3 to go from one side to another. We have to **cross** the road to get to the station.

crow a black bird with a harsh cry.

crowd many people gathered together in one place.

crown a gold and jewelled band worn around the head by a king or queen.

cruel being unkind to a person or an animal.

Cc

crumb a tiny piece of bread or cake.

crust the hard outside part of bread or pie.

cry **1** to be in tears.
2 to shout.

cub the young of some animals. Baby bears, lions and wolves are all **cubs**.

cube a solid shape with six square sides. Dice are **cubes**.

cuckoo a bird which gets its name from the call it makes.

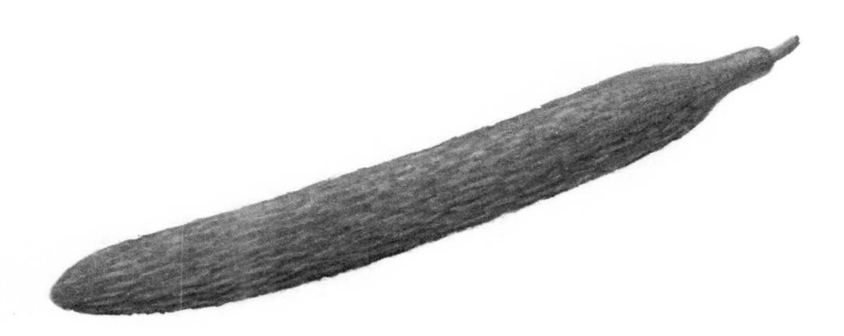

cucumber a long thin green vegetable that is eaten raw.

cupboard a box with shelves and a door. **Cupboards** are used for storing things like food or clothes.

cure to make a sick person better.

curiosity a wish to find something out.

currant a small dried grape used to flavour cakes and buns.

curtain a piece of cloth that hangs in front of a window. **Curtains** can be pulled across the window to cover it.

curve a line that is not straight. A part of a circle is a **curve**.

customer someone who buys something.

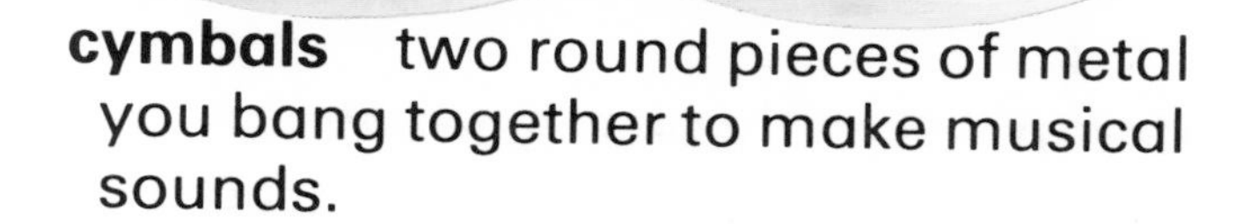

cymbals two round pieces of metal you bang together to make musical sounds.

Dd

daffodil a plant with yellow, bell-shaped flowers.

dagger a sharp, pointed knife, like a short sword.

daily every day. We have a **daily** newspaper.

dairy a place where milk or milk products like butter and cream are stored and sold.

daisy a small wild flower with little white petals around a yellow centre.

dam a bank of earth or concrete built to hold back water.

damp slightly wet. If you wear **damp** clothes you may get a cold.

dance to move in time to music.

dandelion a wild flower with yellow petals, often growing in grassy fields or lawns.

danger something not safe which could harm or hurt you.

dare to be brave enough to do or say something. I would not **dare** dive from the top board at the swimming pool.

dark without any light. It is difficult to see in the **dark**.

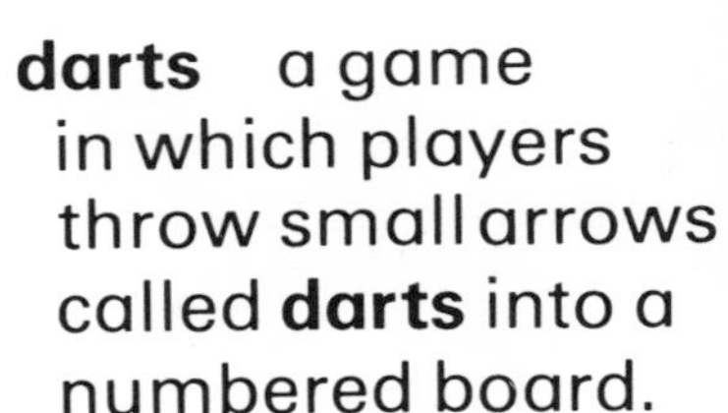

darts a game in which players throw small arrows called **darts** into a numbered board.

date **1** a day in the year shown as a number and a month. January 1st is a **date**.
2 the fruit of a palm tree.

daughter a girl or woman who is the child of two people.

dawn early in the morning when it begins to be light.

day the 24 hours between one midnight and the next.

dazzle to shine a very bright light in someone's eyes, so that they cannot see properly.

dead not living.

deaf not able to hear.

dear 1 much loved or liked.
2 costing a lot of money to buy.

decimal a way of showing numbers and parts of numbers in mathematics. 0.5 is a **decimal** that means a half. (See also *fraction*).

decorations things used to make a room or tree look colourful. Paper chains, balloons and flags are **decorations**.

deep a long way down. The river is **deep** in the middle.

deer a grass-eating animal with antlers. **Deer** run fast when they are attacked.

delicious very nice to taste and eat. That was a **delicious** meal.

denim strong cotton cloth for clothes, like jeans and skirts.

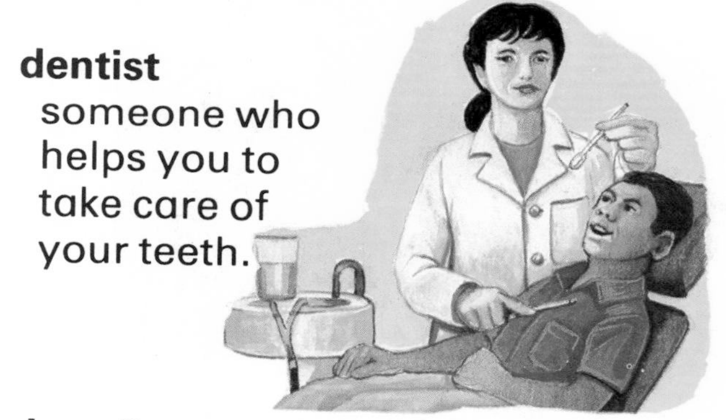

dentist someone who helps you to take care of your teeth.

describe to give a picture of somebody or something in words.

desert a dry sandy area of land where few plants or trees can grow.

deserve to be worthy of. Jane **deserved** the prize because she won the race.

Dd

desk a table you sit at to read or write.

dessert something sweet you eat after the main course of a meal.

destroy to ruin. The fire **destroyed** the house.

detective a police officer who tries to solve crimes.

devil a very bad spirit who is the enemy of God.

dew drops of water sometimes covering the ground early in the morning.

diamond a hard, clear, bright stone that is very valuable. My mother has a **diamond** ring.

diary a book with lined sheets of paper in which you write down what you do every day.

dice a cube of wood or bone which has one to six spots on its six sides. **Dice** are often used with board games.

dictionary a book like this one with words in alphabetical order with their meanings.

different not the same. Paul's hair is a **different** colour from Jill's.

difficult not easy to do or understand.

dig to make a hole in the earth with a spade.

digger a machine that moves large amounts of earth. (See *machines* – page 78)

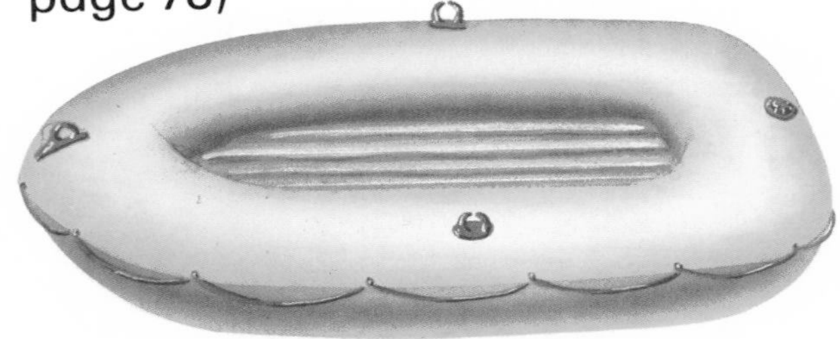

dinghy a small open rowing boat or sailing boat.

dining room the room where you eat your meals.

dinner the main meal of the day. Some people have **dinner** in the middle of the day, others have it in the evening.

dinosaur a very big animal that lived millions of years ago. (See page 44)

dirty not clean.

disaster something terrible that happens without warning.

disco a room or hall where young people can dance to pop records.

disease any illness which comes from catching germs.

dish a kind of plate or bowl with a rim.

dive to jump head first into deep water.

divide to split up into parts or shares. We **divided** the money between the two of us.

dock a place by the edge of the sea or a river where ships are loaded and unloaded.

doctor someone who takes care of you when you are unwell.

dog a four-legged animal usually kept as a pet. A terrier is one of many breeds of **dog**. (See *animals* – page 11)

doll a toy that looks like a baby or child.

dollar money used in several countries, like Australia, Canada and the United States of America.

dolphin a sea animal which can perform tricks.

dominoes a game played using oblong tiles with a different number of spots on each one.

dinosaurs
ichthyosaurus
pterodactyl
triceratops
stegosaurus
tyrannosaurus
brontosaurus

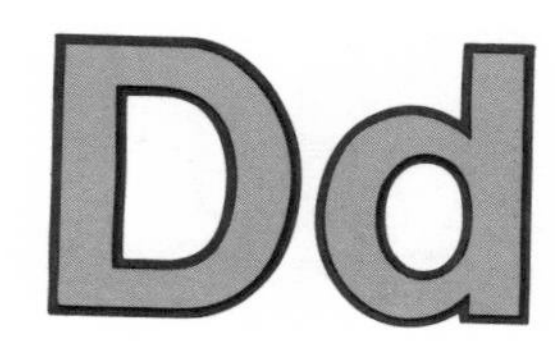

donkey an animal like a pony with long ears.

door an entrance into a room or building that opens and shuts.

double twice as much. Eight is **double** four.

doughnut a round cake of heavy floury mixture, coated with sugar. **Doughnuts** usually have jam or cream in them.

dove a bird like a pigeon. (See *birds* – page 19)

dozen another word for twelve, or a group of twelve things.

dragon a fairy-tale animal with wings, which breathes fire.

dragonfly a flying insect with two pairs of wings. **Dragonflies** live near rivers and lakes.

drain a pipe under the ground carrying waste water away from a building.

draw 1 to make a picture using pencils or crayons.
2 to score the same number of points in a game as your opponent.

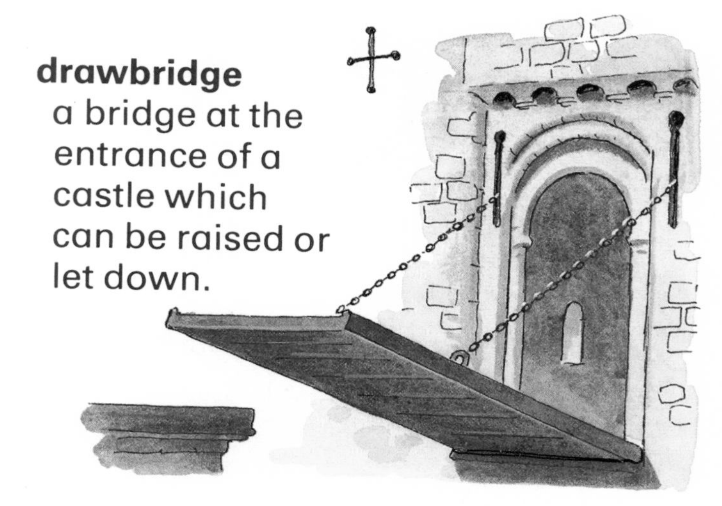

drawbridge a bridge at the entrance of a castle which can be raised or let down.

drawer a box that slides in and out of a desk or chest.

dream to see pictures in your mind when you are asleep. Last night I **dreamed** I was driving a train.

dress 1 a piece of clothing worn by women and girls.
2 to put on your clothes.

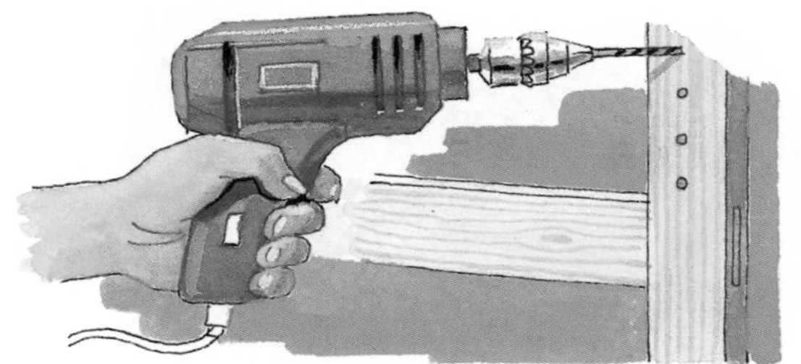

drill a tool for making holes in things.

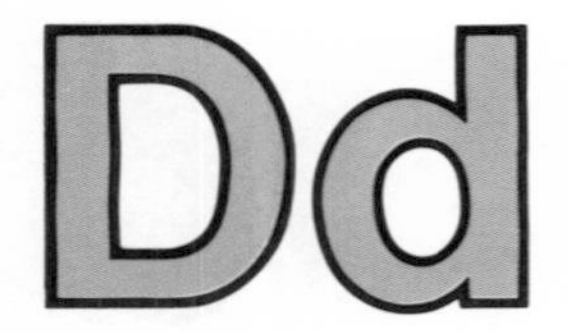

drink to swallow a liquid.

driver a person who works the controls of a vehicle to make it go.

drop to let something fall. Anne **dropped** a stone into the pond.

drown to die by staying under water too long.

drum a musical instrument that you beat with sticks in time to music.

dry not wet. For three days the weather has been **dry** and very sunny.

duck a bird with a flat beak and webbed feet, that swims and flies.

duffel coat a thick woolly coat with a hood and loop fasteners.

dull not bright or not interesting. The weather was **dull** and the game was **dull**.

dumb not able or not willing to speak.

dummy a piece of rubber that babies suck to comfort them.

dungeon a prison cell in or underneath an old building like a castle.

dustbin a metal or plastic container with a lid, to hold rubbish.

duvet (sounds like doo – vay) a large bag of feathers used flat on a bed as a cover.

dwarf a small person. In the fairy tale, Snow White met seven **dwarfs**.

dynamite a powerful chemical mixture used for blowing up buildings, or rocks in a quarry.

Ee

eagle a large fierce bird with a sharp curved beak.

ear one of the two flaps of skin on the sides of your head that you hear with.

early 1 in good time. We get up **early** in the morning to catch the 8 o'clock bus for school.
2 sooner than expected.

earth 1 the planet we live on.
2 soil.

earthquake a number of shock waves making cracks in the earth's surface. **Earthquakes** can cause buildings to fall down.

easel a stand to hold up a painting.

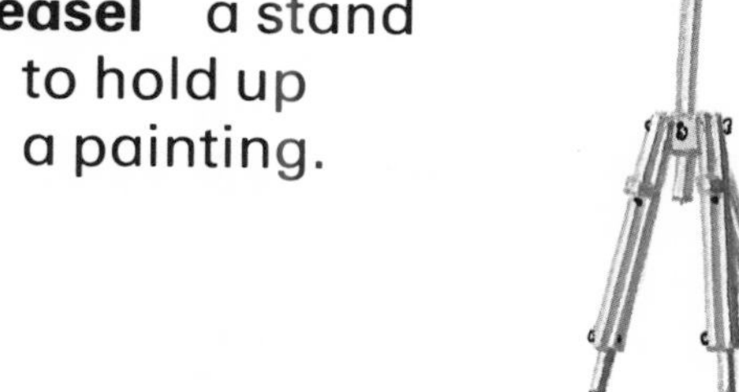

easy not difficult to do or to understand. The sums in class today were **easy**.

eat to chew and swallow food.

echo a sound that bounces back to you in a cave or tunnel or in some buildings.

eclipse the shutting out of light in the sky when the moon comes between the earth and the sun.

edge the end or rim of something.

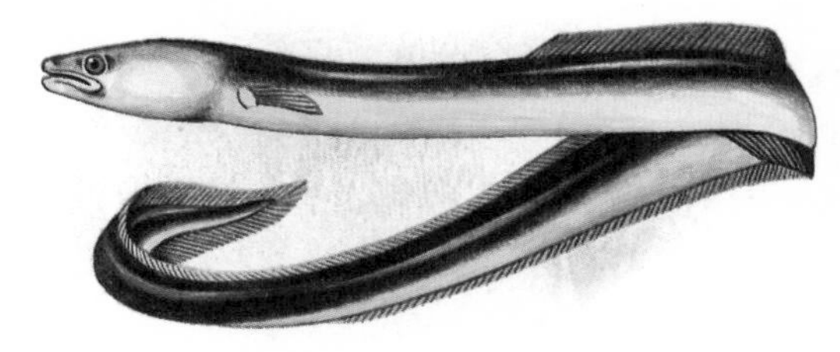

eel a long snake-like fish.

egg some animal babies are hatched from **eggs**. Hens lay **eggs** that we cook and eat.

elastic a material made with rubber which stretches when you pull it and springs back when you let go.

elbow the place where your arm bends.

electricity a form of power which flows along wires to give light or heat, or drive machines.

Ee

elephant a very large grey animal with huge flapping ears and a long tube-like nose, called a trunk.

elf a small, mischievous fellow found in fairy tales. Some **elves** have magical powers.

emerald a bright green stone of great value used in jewellery.

emigrate to leave your own country and go to live in another country.

emperor someone who rules over a number of countries.

empty having nothing in it.

emu a large Australian bird which cannot fly but can run fast.

encyclopedia a large book, or set of books, which tells you about many things.

end **1** the last bit of something.
2 to put a stop to; to finish.

enemy someone who fights against you.

energy the power or strength to work or play.

engine a machine that makes something work. Cars have **engines** to make them go.

enjoy to be happy with what you are doing. The whole family **enjoyed** the circus.

enormous very big indeed.

enough as much as you need, but no more. Have you had **enough** to eat?

enter **1** to come or go into somewhere.
2 to put in. I **entered** the information into the computer.

entrance the way into a place.

envelope a flat paper container with a sticky flap. **Envelopes** are used for sending letters through the post.

equal the same size or value. Two and two **equals** four.

equator an imaginary line around the middle of the earth.

escape to get away from someone or something. The mouse **escaped** from the cat.

Eskimo a native of the very cold parts of North America and Greenland. **Eskimoes** are also called Innuits.

eve the day before a special day. Christmas **Eve** is the day before Christmas Day.

even 1 flat and smooth.
2 those numbers that are not odd. 2, 4, 6 and 8 are all **even** numbers.
3 level or equal. It was an **even** game that ended in a draw.

evening the part of the day between afternoon and night-time.

exactly absolutely right. It is **exactly** seven o'clock.

exercise 1 to practise the use of your muscles to keep fit.
2 work you do to make you better at something.

explain to make something clear. The teacher **explained** how to use the computer.

explore to go and find out about a new place. We **explored** the caves on the mountainside.

explosion a loud bang made when something blows up.

extraordinary very unusual.

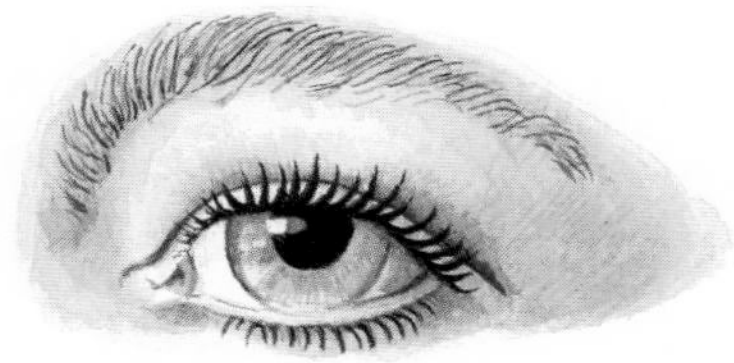

eye we have two **eyes** to see with.

eyebrow the line of hairs above your eyes.

Ff

face the front part of your head.

fact something that has actually happened or is true.

factory a building where things are made, usually with machines.

fair 1 a place with a merry-go-round, stalls and games where you have fun.
2 light in colour.

fairy a small imaginary person with wings who appears in children's stories.

fake a copy made to fool people

fall to drop. The leaves **fall** from the trees in autumn.

false 1 not true.
2 not the real thing. The actor wore a **false** beard.

family father, mother, their children and other relations.

famine a great shortage of food over a wide area. **Famine** in Africa has caused thousands of people to die.

famous very well known. Picasso is a **famous** artist.

fan 1 a shaped piece of wood or paper that people use to cool themselves down.
2 someone who likes a particular team or pop group very much.

farm buildings and fields where a farmer keeps animals or grows food.

farmer someone who owns a farm or runs one for someone else.

father a man who has a child or children of his own.

favourite the one you like best. My **favourite** game is football.

Ff

fear a feeling that someone or something is going to harm you.

feast a big meal of rich food.

feather a piece of the soft coat of a bird. A **feather** is very light and falls slowly to the ground when you drop it.

feeble very weak.

feeling something that you sense inside, like anger, love, pain or joy.

female a woman, or an animal that can have babies.

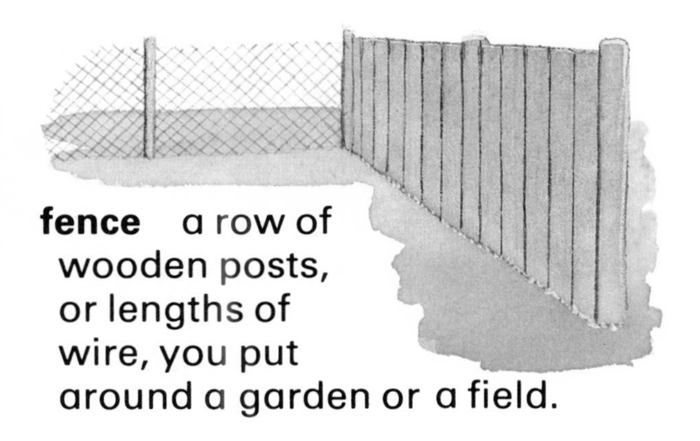

fence a row of wooden posts, or lengths of wire, you put around a garden or a field.

ferry a boat that takes people or cars across a river, lake or sea.

fetch to go and get. Will you **fetch** some wood for the fire?

few not many. **Few** people have climbed Mount Everest.

fidget to move about all the time because you find it hard to keep still.

field an open piece of land, usually in the countryside.

fierce wild and frightening. Our uncle has a **fierce** dog.

fight to struggle with or hit someone.

figure a sign for a number. 1 is a **figure**.

Ff

film 1 something you put in a camera to take photographs.
2 moving pictures you see in a cinema or on television.

final coming at the end of something. December 31st is the **final** day of the year.

find to see something you are looking for.

fine beautiful. It was a **fine** summer's day.

finger a part of the hand. You have four **fingers** and one thumb on each hand.

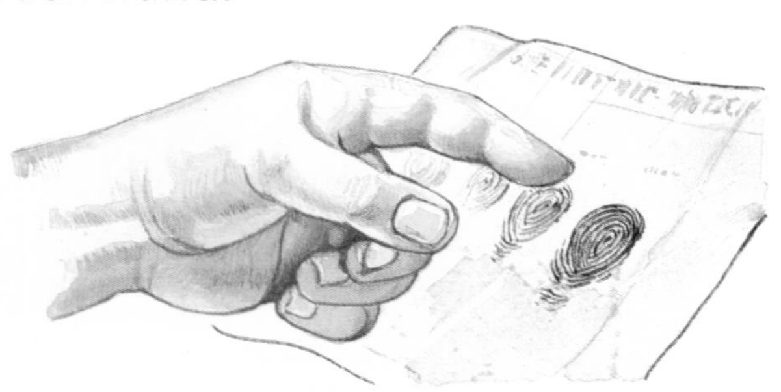

fingerprint the mark left by one of your fingers on the surface of something. The thief left his **fingerprints** all over the door handle.

finish to get to the end. William, please hurry up and **finish** your breakfast.

fire 1 the flames and the heat that come from burning something.
2 to shoot from a gun or from a bow.

fire engine a large vehicle which carries men and equipment to put out a fire.

firework a small tube or packet which burns brightly or explodes into colour when it is lit.

first before anyone or anything else. Jenny came **first** in the 100 metres race.

fish an animal that lives under water all the time, using its fins and tail to swim about.

fisherman someone who catches fish for food or just as a hobby.

fist your hand when the fingers are closed tightly. He hit the table with his **fist**.

fix 1 to mend or repair something. The mechanic **fixed** the car.
2 to arrange. Let's **fix** a date for the party.

fizzy having lots of bubbles that rise to the top. Rosie loves **fizzy** lemonade.

flag a piece of cloth with a coloured pattern. Every country has its own **flag**.

flame the bright tongue of fire that leaps upwards from something burning.

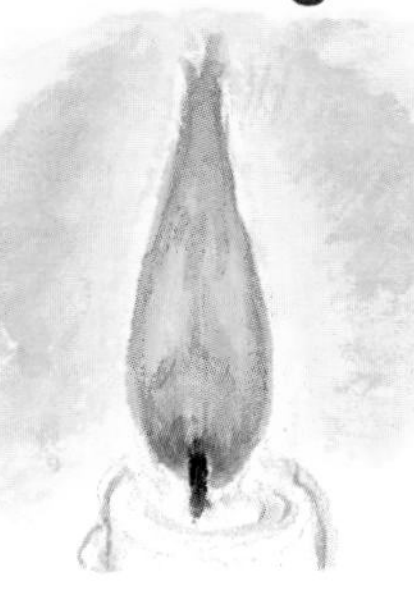

flask a bottle made of metal or plastic for holding drinks.

flavour a special taste in something you eat or drink. That cake has a lemon **flavour**.

flea a very small insect that cannot fly but jumps about.

flight travel through the air, usually of birds or planes.

flippers 1 big rubber flat-toed shoes which help you to swim.
2 the limbs of some creatures. Seals and dolphins have **flippers**.

float to rest on the surface of water or in space without falling. The lumberjacks let the logs **float** down the river.

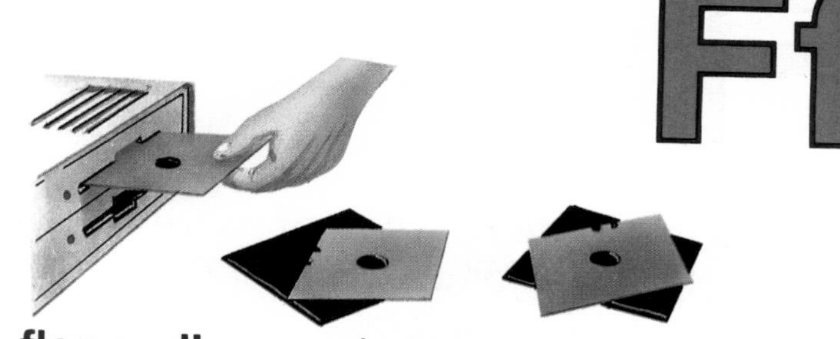

floppy disc a plastic disc that contains information. **Floppy discs** are used in computers.

flour white or brown powder that comes from crushed grain. **Flour** is used to make bread and cakes.

flower the part of a plant that holds the seeds. **Flowers** are often bright colours.

flute a musical instrument made of wood or metal. You play the **flute** by holding it sideways and blowing across a hole.

fly 1 to move through the air.
2 a small winged insect.

foal a young horse at birth or during its first year.

fog a thick mist or cloud near the ground.

fold to bend into two or more parts. George **folded** the letter and put it in an envelope.

follow to come after something. B **follows** A in the alphabet.

food what we eat to stay alive.

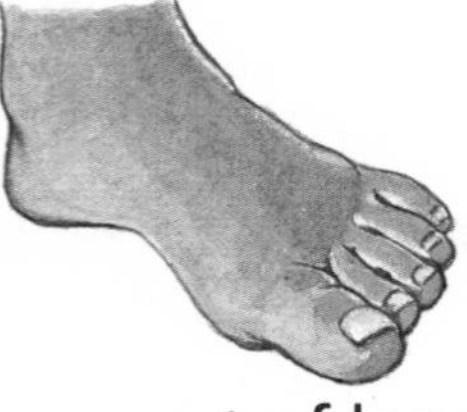

foot **1** the part of your body at the lower end of your leg.
2 a measurement of length. One **foot** is just over 30 centimetres.

football **1** a game played by two teams of 11 people who try to kick or head a ball into their opponents' goal. (See *sports* – page 128)
2 the ball used in the game of football.

footpath a narrow track for people to walk along.

forehead part of your face above your eyes.

forest a large group of trees growing close together.

forget not able to remember. My sister **forgot** to give her friend a birthday present.

forgive to accept it when someone says they are sorry for upsetting you.

fork **1** a tool with prongs you use for eating food with.
2 a tool for digging and weeding in the garden.

fort a strong building with high walls where soldiers live and work.

fortnight two weeks. We went on holiday for a **fortnight**.

fortune **1** your good or bad luck in the future. The gypsy told us our **fortunes**.
2 a large amount of money.

forward to the front. Step **forward** all those who want to play.

fossil part of a prehistoric animal or plant marked in a piece of stone.

fountain a jet of water pushed up into the air.

fox a wild animal with a long bushy tail.

fraction a part or amount of something. In mathematics, **fractions** are shown as numbers. ½ is a **fraction** that means a half.

freckle a small brown mark people sometimes have on their skin. Some people get **freckles** after being in the sun too long.

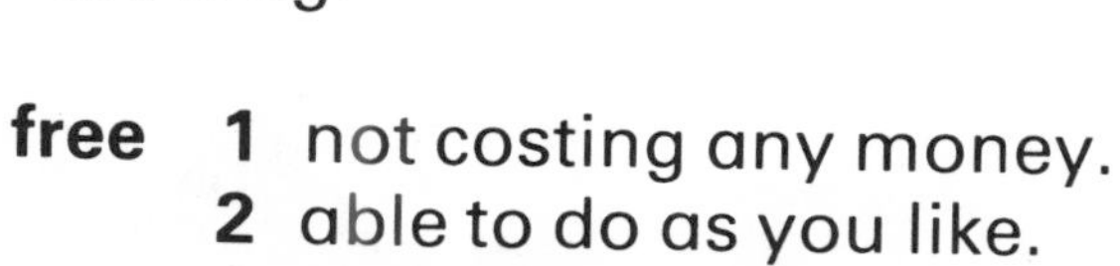

free 1 not costing any money.
2 able to do as you like.
3 not a prisoner.

freeze to become hard in the cold weather. Water **freezes** to ice when it is very cold.

fresh just made; new. I like the smell of **fresh** bread straight from the oven.

friend someone you know and like a lot.

frighten to make afraid. My sister is **frightened** by spiders.

frog a small web-footed animal that lives in or near water and moves about by jumping.

front the first or most forward part. Tom was at the **front** of the queue for the cinema.

frost a thin white covering on the ground when it is very cold. Our plants were damaged by **frost** last winter.

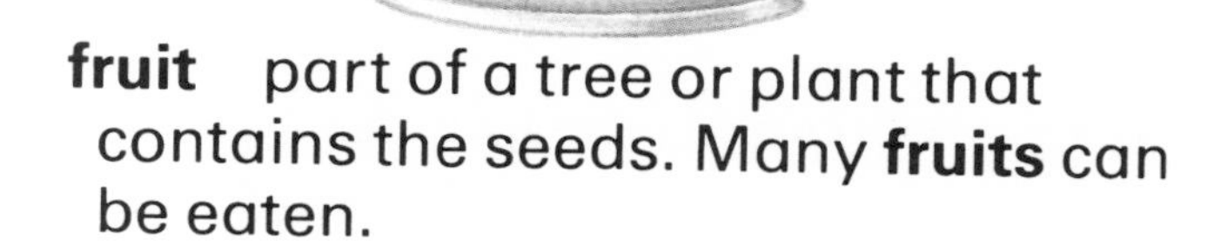

fruit part of a tree or plant that contains the seeds. Many **fruits** can be eaten.

funny something that makes you laugh. Do you know any **funny** jokes?

fur the soft coat of hair on many animals.

fuselage the main body of an aeroplane.

galaxy a very large group of planets and stars. Our solar system is part of the **galaxy** called the Milky Way.

gale a very strong wind.

galleon a sailing ship of long ago with three masts.

gallon a measurement of liquids. One **gallon** is about the same as 4½ litres.

game something you play using a number of rules.

gang a group of people doing something together. Billy the Kid joined a **gang** of outlaws.

garage 1 a building where you keep a car or cars.
2 a place where cars are sold or mended.
3 a place where petrol is sold.

garden a piece of land by your house where grass, flowers, fruit and vegetables grow.

gargle to wash your throat by bubbling liquid around at the back of your mouth.

gas an invisible substance like air. Some **gases** can be burned. We heat our house with **gas** central heating.

gate a door in a fence or hedge.

gazelle a small antelope with big beautiful eyes.

general 1 one of the top ranks of officer in the army.
2 usual.

Gg

geography the study of countries, seas, rivers, mountains and lakes.

geology the study of the earth and its rocks.

germ a tiny living thing that can only be seen under a microscope. Some **germs** make people ill if they get into the bloodstream.

ghost the spirit of a person who has died. Some people believe that **ghosts** return to where they once lived.

giant a huge, powerful and often bad person in a fairy story.

gigantic very, very big.

giraffe a very tall wild animal with long legs and a long neck.

glacier a huge mass of ice that moves down a mountainside.

glass **1** a hard material you can see through.
2 a container made of glass you can drink from.

glasses another word for spectacles. John wears **glasses** to see things more clearly.

glider a lightweight aeroplane with no engine. A **glider** is pulled into the air by another plane, and let go to glide down to the ground.

glitter to shine brightly. The diamonds **glittered** in the Queen's crown.

globe a large ball which has a map of the world on it.

glove a cover for your hand, with separate places for your fingers.

glue a strong wet paste used for sticking things.

gnome in fairy stories, an ugly dwarf that lives under the ground.

goal the name of the scoring point in football when your team gets the ball into your opponents' net.

goat a four-legged animal like a sheep with horns.

gobble to eat very quickly and make lots of noise about it.

go-kart a small simple racing car with a frame, four wheels and a small engine.

gold a shiny yellow metal that is very valuable.

goldfish a small orange fish you keep in a tank or in a pond as a pet.

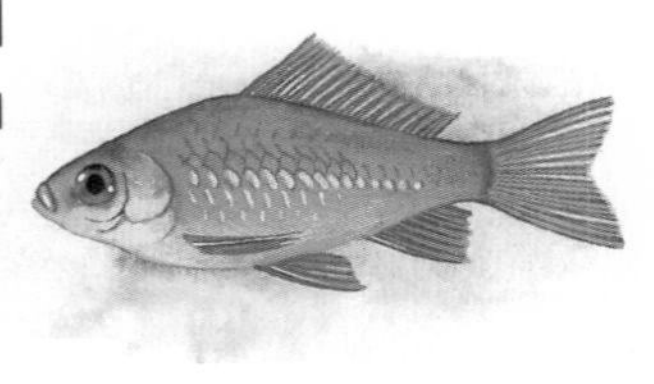

golf an outdoor game played using a small white ball and a set of sticks called clubs. (See *sports* – page 128)

goose a large bird like a duck with a long neck. (See *birds* – page 19)

gooseberry a small green fruit with a hairy skin.

gorilla a large African ape.

grab to snatch. The thief **grabbed** the money-bag.

grain the seeds of some plants we use as food, like rice or wheat.

gramme a very small measure of weight. There are 1,000 **grammes** in one kilogramme.

grape a red, yellow or purple fruit that grows in bunches on a vine. Wine is made from crushed **grapes**.

grapefruit a yellow fruit like a big orange often eaten for breakfast.

grasshopper a small jumping insect which makes a clicking noise with its legs.

great 1 very large.
2 important.

greedy wanting more than you need. The **greedy** bear ate too much honey.

greenhouse a building made of glass where you grow plants that need extra warmth.

ground the earth and soil we walk on. Julie slipped off her bicycle and fell to the **ground** with a bump.

group a number of people or things together. A **group** of people came round last night to sing carols.

grow 1 to get bigger. George has **grown** as tall as his brother.
2 to plant seeds in the soil and care for them.

growl the sound made by some kinds of animal when angry or frightened.

guard 1 someone who protects other people or things.
2 to keep safe.

guess to give an answer to a question without being certain it is correct. How old are you? I **guess** you are eight.

guide 1 to show someone the way to a place.
2 a person who shows other people the way or leads them.

guinea pig a small furry animal with no tail, often kept as a pet.

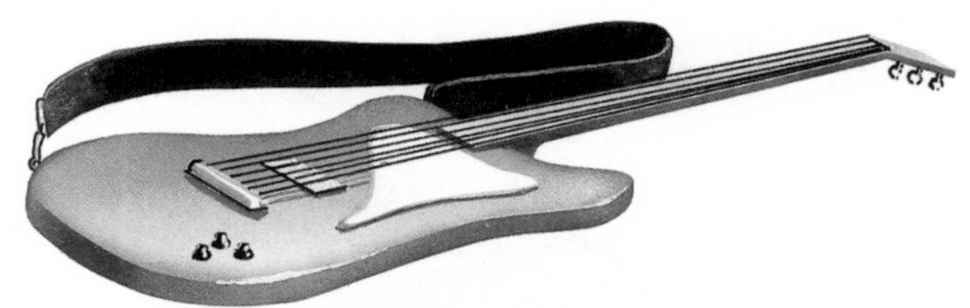

guitar a musical instrument with six strings. Most rock groups use electric **guitars**.

gunpowder a black powder that explodes when set on fire.

habit something you do very often without thinking.

haircut having your hair trimmed by a hairdresser.

half one of two equal parts that a whole thing can be divided into.

Hallowe'en the night of October 31st, when you dress up as a witch or a ghost and play tricks on people.

hamburger a flat round piece of chopped meat fried and often served in a bun.

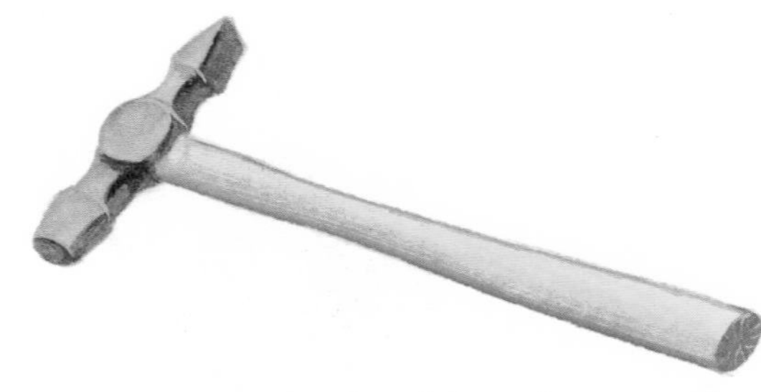

hammer a tool with a heavy head for hitting nails or for breaking things.

hamster a small furry animal with a short tail. Some people keep **hamsters** as pets.

handbag a small bag for holding useful things like money and keys. Some people carry **handbags** when they go out.

handcuffs a pair of metal rings a police officer uses to hold a criminal's wrists together.

handkerchief a small piece of cloth you use for blowing or wiping your nose.

handle the part of a cup or tool you hold when you pick it up.

handlebars the part of a bicycle you hold to steer it along the road.

hangar a large shed where aeroplanes are kept.

hanger a curved bar or frame you use to hang clothes on.

happen to take place. An accident **happened** at the end of our street this morning.

Hh

harbour a sheltered place on the coast where the water is deep enough for ships to stay.

hard 1 difficult. These questions are **hard** to answer.
2 not soft. The ground was **hard** after the frost today.

hare an animal like a rabbit with long ears and big feet. **Hares** can run fast.

harm to hurt or damage.

harp a musical instrument with strings you pluck with your fingers.

harvest the time of year when farmers gather their crops.

hatch 1 to be born from an egg by breaking out of the shell.
2 a movable cover in a wall, roof or floor that you can open and close.

haystack a tidy pile of dried grass used to feed animals.

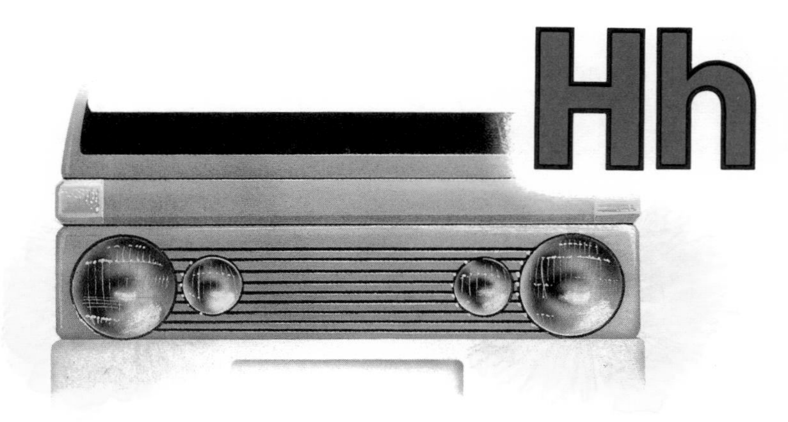

headlights the bright lights on the front of a vehicle.

healthy being well.

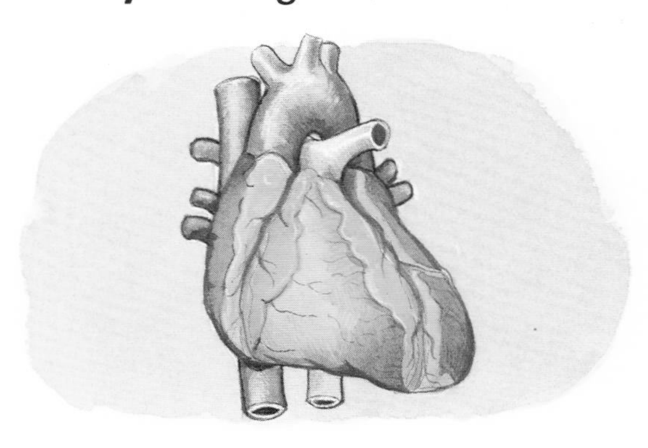

heart the part of your body which pumps your blood.

heat 1 to make something hot.
2 warmth.

Heaven the home of God.

heavy difficult to pick up; weighing a lot.

hedge a row of bushes that grow very close together to form a wall around a field or garden.

hedgehog a small animal covered with stiff, prickly hairs.

Hh

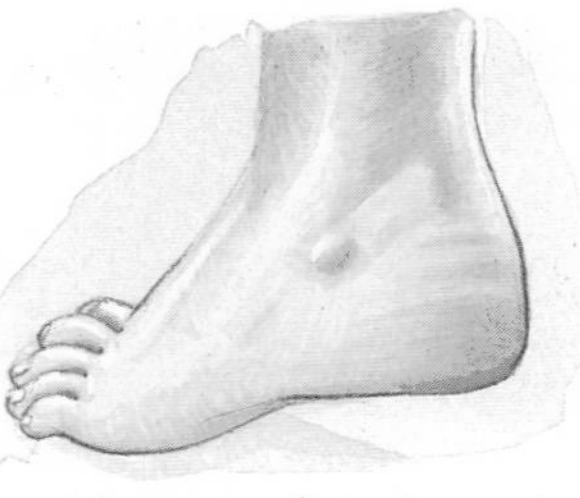

heel the back part of your foot.

height the distance from the top to the bottom of something. Nicola's **height** is 130 centimetres.

helicopter an aircraft that has rotating blades on top. **Helicopters** can fly straight up in the air.

helmet a hat specially made to protect the head. Motorcycle riders wear **helmets**.

help to make something easier for somebody to do. The teacher **helped** my brother with his handwriting.

heron a bird with long legs that lives near rivers or lakes.

hide 1 to go where you cannot be seen.
2 to put something where no one can find it.

hill a part of the land higher than the ground around it.

hip the bone that sticks out just below your waist.

hippopotamus a very large thick-skinned water animal that lives in Africa.

history the story of things that happened in the past.

hit 1 to strike. She **hit** her arm on the table.
2 a popular song or record.

hive a wooden box made for bees to live in.

hobby something you enjoy doing in your free time. Jane's **hobby** is collecting stamps.

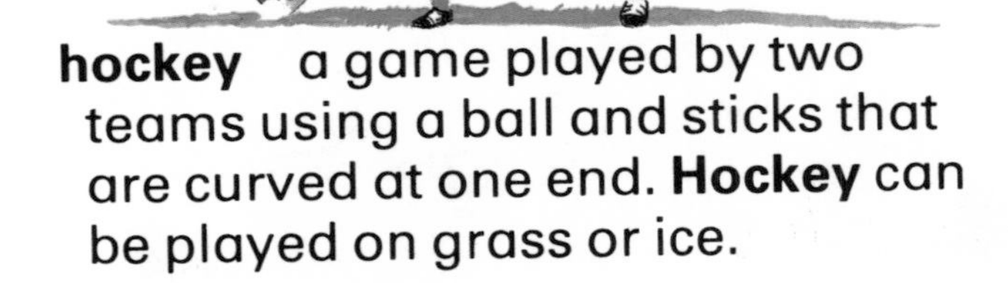

hockey a game played by two teams using a ball and sticks that are curved at one end. **Hockey** can be played on grass or ice.

hole an opening in or through something. The mouse disappeared down a **hole** in the ground.

holiday a time when you do not go to work or school.

holly an evergreen bush with prickly leaves and red berries.

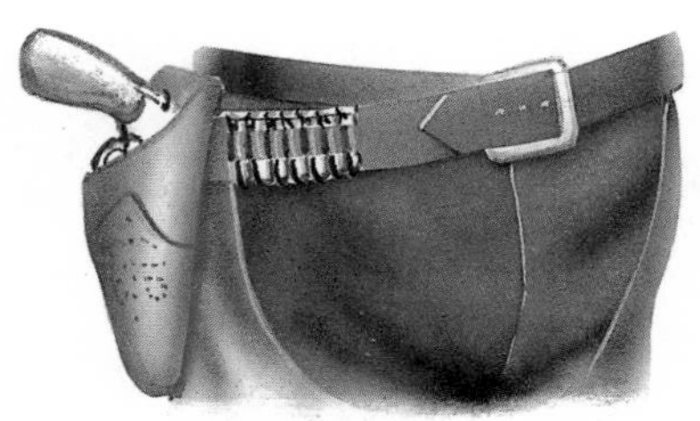

holster a leather case for putting a gun in. Some cowboys wear a **holster** on a belt around their waist.

homework work for school that you do at home in the evening.

honey a sweet, sticky food made by bees. You can eat **honey** on bread.

hood a warm covering for your head and neck often joined on to a coat.

hoof the hard part of some animals' feet. Horses and donkeys have **hoofs**.

hook a bent, pointed piece of metal for hanging things on or for catching things like fish.

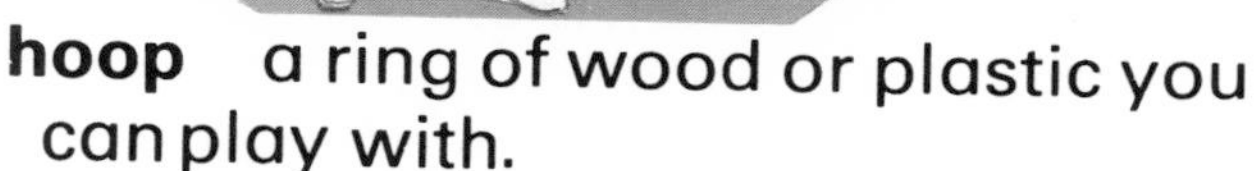

hoop a ring of wood or plastic you can play with.

hope to wish that something will happen. I do **hope** you will come to my birthday party next week.

hopscotch a hopping game where you throw a stone into squares drawn on the ground.

horn **1** a hard pointed bone coming out of the top of the head of some animals. Goats and sheep have **horns**.
2 a musical instrument.

horse a large animal with four legs and hoofs. (See *animals* – page 11)

horseshoe the curved flat piece of metal a blacksmith nails on to a horse's hoof.

hose a long, rubber or plastic pipe used for watering the garden.

Hh

hospital a place where sick or injured people are taken care of by doctors and nurses.

hotel a building where people stay and pay for a bedroom and meals.

hour a measure of time. There are 60 minutes in an **hour**. There are 24 **hours** in a day.

house a building that people live in. We have a **house** near the river.

hovercraft a vehicle which travels on a cushion of air over water or land.

huge very large.

hummingbird a small brightly coloured bird that makes a humming sound by beating its wings very fast.

hungry needing food. We were all **hungry** when we got home.

hunt **1** to look carefully for something.
2 to chase and try to catch something. Leopards **hunt** antelope for food.

hurricane a storm with very strong winds.

hurry to go or move quickly; to rush. **Hurry** to catch the train or you will miss it!

hurt to cause injury or pain. I fell over and **hurt** my knee.

husband a man who is married.

hut a small simple building used for shelter.

hutch a small cage for pets. Johnny keeps his two white rabbits in a **hutch**.

hyena a wild animal that looks like a dog and hunts for its food. Some **hyenas** have a call like a loud laugh.

ice frozen water. We like **ice** with our drinks to keep them cold.

iceberg a large mass of ice that floats in the sea.

ice box the very cold part of a refrigerator where ice is made.

ice cream a cold, sweet food. There are many flavours of **ice cream**.

ice skating a sport where you glide over ice wearing special boots with a sharp blade underneath.

icicle a sharp piece of ice made from dripping water. **Icicles** hang down from roofs or gutters in freezing weather.

idle not working ; lazy.

igloo a house Eskimoes build from blocks of frozen snow.

ill not feeling well.

illustration a picture that helps explain words in a book. There are five **illustrations** on this page.

imagination making pictures in your mind about things or people.

important having a lot of value or worth a lot of attention.

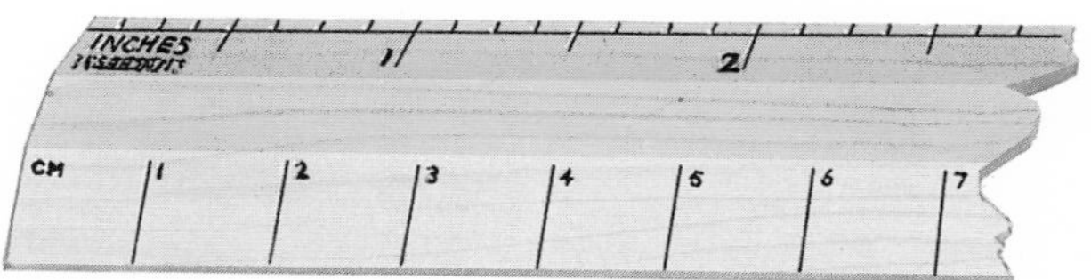

inch a measure of length. There are 12 **inches** in one foot.

indoors inside a building. My cat stays **indoors** when it rains.

infectious likely to spread germs to other people. Sally has chicken-pox and will be **infectious** for a few days.

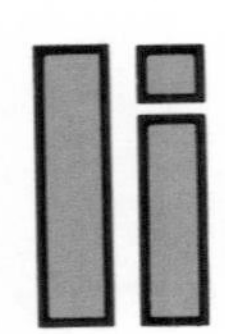

information facts or news. I went to the library to get some **information** about dinosaurs.

ink a coloured liquid used for writing or printing.

inquisitive fond of asking questions.

insect a small creature with six legs. A fly is an **insect**.

inside on the inner side. He opened the door and went **inside** the house.

inspector 1 a police officer in charge of other policemen.
2 someone who examines things to check they are working properly.

instead in place of. Joan sent her mother a postcard **instead** of a letter.

instrument 1 a tool you use to make or repair something.
2 something you play to make musical sounds.

invention a new machine or tool made for the first time ever.

invisible something which is there but which you cannot see. The magician cast a spell and made himself **invisible**.

invitation asking someone to a meal or a party.

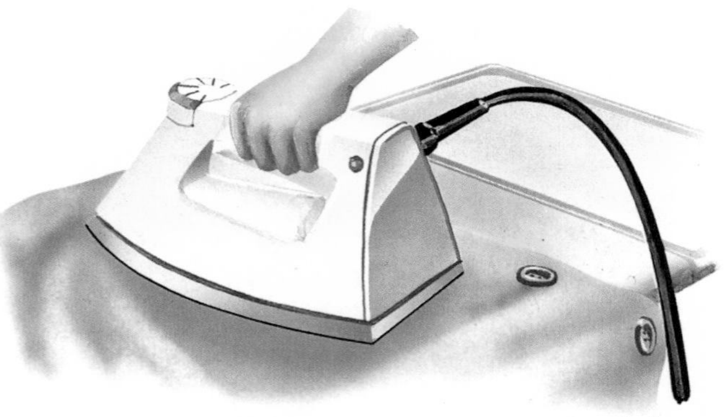

iron 1 a flat piece of metal with a handle. You make the **iron** hot and rub it over clothes to smooth out creases.
2 a strong grey metal.

island a piece of land with water all around it.

itch a tickling feeling in your skin that makes you want to scratch it.

ivy a green climbing plant with shiny leaves. The front wall of our house is covered with **ivy**.

jack a tool used for lifting heavy things like cars off the ground.

jackal a wild animal that looks like a dog.

jacket a short coat with sleeves.

jack-in-the-box a toy which looks like a box. When the lid is opened a funny figure jumps out.

jaguar a large spotted animal of the cat family that runs very fast and lives in South America.

jam **1** a sweet food made with fruit. You can spread **jam** on bread or cakes.
2 people or vehicles packed together so they cannot move. We were stuck in a traffic **jam** on the way home yesterday.

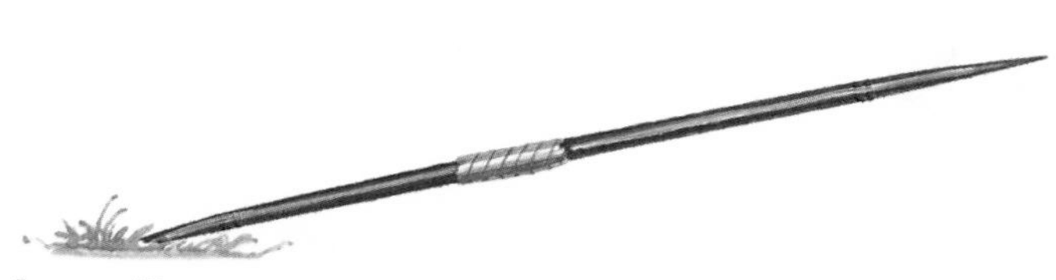

javelin a spear for throwing in sports.

jaw the upper or lower bone of the mouth holding your teeth.

jazz a popular style of music invented by American negro musicians.

jeans strong trousers made of heavy cloth.

jeep a strong four-wheeled vehicle with a powerful engine. **Jeeps** are often used by the army to travel over rough ground.

jellyfish a sea creature with a soft body shaped like an umbrella.

jet **1** a fast aeroplane driven by forcing hot gas backwards out of the engine.
2 water or gas squirted by force.

jewel a precious stone of great value. Diamonds and emeralds are **jewels**.

jigsaw puzzle a picture made of wood or cardboard that is cut into uneven pieces. You must put the pieces together to make the picture.

jingle 1 a sound like small bells ringing together.
2 a simple catchy tune.

jockey someone who rides a horse in a race.

jogger someone who runs at a slow steady pace for exercise.

joke a funny story told in a few words.

journalist a person who writes articles or news reports in newspapers and magazines.

journey a long trip to or from a place.

judge a person who decides who is right in an argument or decides who has won a competition.

juggler someone who can throw, catch and balance several things at once.

juice the liquid part of a fruit or vegetable.

juke box a machine that plays pop records when you put money in it.

jumble a mixture of things in a muddle.

jumper a knitted woollen pullover with long sleeves.

junction the place where two or more roads or railway lines cross. We always take care when we cycle across a road **junction**.

jungle a thick forest found in hot countries.

junk old things of little value.

Kk

kangaroo an Australian animal that jumps along on strong back legs. Female **kangaroos** have a pouch to carry their babies.

kayak an Eskimo canoe made out of wood and animal skins.

keen very interested or excited to do something. Mark is **keen** to have swimming lessons.

keep to have or look after. David's father **keeps** chickens in the back garden.

kerb the edge of a pavement.

kettle a metal pot for boiling water. A **kettle** has a handle and a spout.

kettledrum a musical instrument that is a large drum.

key **1** a small piece of metal you open a lock with.
2 a part of some instruments and machines which you press with your fingers. Pianos and typewriters have **keys**.

kick to hit something with your foot.

kill to put someone or something to death.

kilogramme a measure of weight. There are 1000 grammes in one **kilogramme**.

kilometre a measure of length. There are 1000 metres in one **kilometre**.

kilt a coloured, pleated skirt usually worn in Scotland by men and women. The **kilt** is part of Scotland's national costume.

kind **1** good towards other people.
2 a sort. A daisy is a **kind** of flower.

king a man who rules a country.

kingdom a country or group of countries ruled by a king or queen.

Kk

kingfisher a small brightly coloured bird that lives near water.

kiss to touch someone with your lips to show you like them.

kitchen the room where food is cooked.

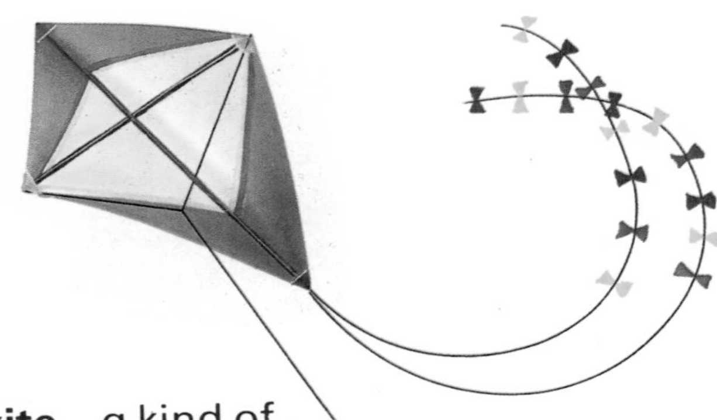

kite a kind of toy that flies in the wind at the end of a long string.

kitten a young cat.

kiwi a New Zealand bird that has very short wings and cannot fly.

knee the middle part of your leg where it bends.

knife a sharp metal blade with a handle. **Knives** are used for cutting.

knight someone in olden times who wore armour and fought on horseback.

knit to make wool into clothes using long needles.

knob a round handle on a drawer or a door.

knock to hit something. My brother **knocked** on my bedroom door before coming in.

knot the twisted part where pieces of string or rope are tied together.

knowledge things you know about. Kate has a good general **knowledge**.

koala a furry Australian animal like a small bear.

label a piece of paper fixed to something saying who it belongs to or what it is.

lace **1** fine cloth with a pattern of holes.
2 a kind of string for tying shoes.

ladder a set of steps for climbing. **Ladders** are made of two long pieces of wood or metal with small pieces, called rungs, between them.

ladybird a small flying insect which is red or yellow with black spots.

lair the den of a wild animal.

lake a large amount of water with land all around it.

lamb a young sheep.

lamp post a tall metal or concrete post with a lamp on top to light up a street.

land **1** the parts of our planet that are not covered with water.
2 to arrive at a place by ship or aeroplane. We **landed** at London Airport.

language the words used by people of different countries. You can learn to speak a foreign **language** at school.

lantern a light in a case made of metal and glass.

lap **1** the part of your body from your waist to your knees when you are sitting down.
2 once around a race track.

lark a small brown bird that sings sweetly.

laser an instrument that can send out a thin but powerful beam of light.

lasso (sounds like lassoo) a length of rope with a sliding loop. Cowboys use a **lasso** to catch horses and cattle.

late happening or arriving after the expected time.

laughter the sound you make when someone says or does something funny.

Ll

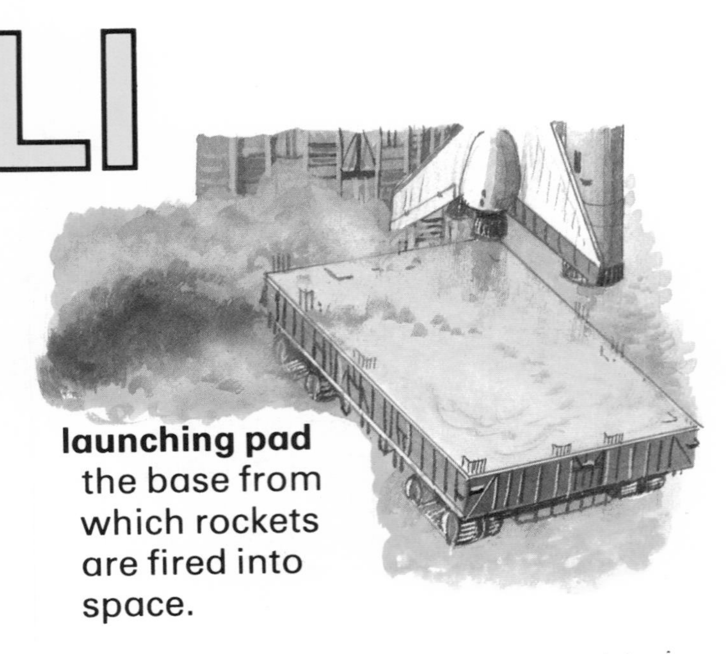

launching pad the base from which rockets are fired into space.

launderette a place with washing machines and tumble driers where people pay to wash and dry their clothes.

lava very hot rock that flows as liquid out of an erupting volcano.

lawnmower a machine that cuts grass. (See *machines* – page 78)

lay **1** to make eggs. The farmer's hens **lay** brown eggs.
2 to put down. Two people came to **lay** the carpet.

lazy not wanting to work.

lead
1 (sounds like led) a heavy grey metal.
2 (sounds like leed) to be at the front or to show the way.

leader someone who is the head of a group of people.

leaf one of the flat green bits that grow on trees and plants.

leapfrog a game where one person jumps over another from behind.

leap year a year that has an extra day in it. A **leap year** happens once every four years when there are 29 days in February instead of 28.

learn to get to know something. We **learn** to write at school.

least the smallest amount.

leather the dried skin of some animals used to make things. My shoes are made of **leather**.

leave to go away from a person or place. I am **leaving** school at the end of the year.

leek a vegetable like an onion, with a long white stem and green leaves.

left the opposite to right. Your heart is on the **left** side of your body.

leg one of the two parts of your body you stand or walk on.

legend an old story believed by people long ago and passed down to us today.

lemon a fruit like an orange with a yellow skin. **Lemons** have a sour taste.

lemonade a drink made from lemons, sugar and water. **Lemonade** is usually fizzy.

length the distance from one end to another. 50 metres is the **length** of an Olympic swimming pool.

leopard a fierce wild animal of the cat family which lives in Africa and Asia. **Leopards** have yellow skin with black spots.

leotard a piece of clothing that fits close to the body and is worn by acrobats and dancers.

less not so much; a smaller amount or number. My sister has been eating **less** after her illness.

lesson the time given each day to learning about each subject.

letter **1** a message you write on paper and send to someone.
2 a part of the alphabet like a or j or q.

lettuce a vegetable with large green leaves that you eat raw.

library a room or a building filled with books you can borrow and read.

lick to make something wet with your tongue. You have to **lick** a stamp to stick it on an envelope.

lie 1 to rest in a flat position.
2 something you say which you know is not true.

life the time when you are alive.

lifeboat a special boat that saves people at sea.

lift 1 to pick something up.
2 a machine that carries people up and down a building. A **lift** looks like a small room.

light 1 not heavy.
2 something that shines so you can see in the dark.
3 to make something burn.

lighthouse a tall tower by the coast with a flashing light on top that guides ships in the dark.

lightning the flashes of bright light seen in the sky during a thunderstorm.

like 1 to be fond of. I **like** strawberries and cream.
2 almost the same. John looks **like** his father.

line 1 a long thin mark on a page.
2 a row of people or things.

liner a large ship for passengers going on long voyages.

lion a wild animal of the cat family found in Africa and India. Male **lions** have a large mane. (See *animals* – page 11)

lip 1 the front edge of your mouth. You have a top **lip** and a bottom **lip**.
2 the edge of a cup or glass.

lipstick a soft, coloured stick that looks like a crayon. You use **lipstick** to brighten your lips.

liquid anything wet that can be poured. Water and milk are **liquids**.

liquorice a black sweet made from the root of the **liquorice** plant.

listen to pay attention to hear something. Bobby **listened** carefully to the words of the song.

litre a measure of quantity for liquids. One **litre** is a little less than two pints.

little small; not much.

living alive. My grandfather is still **living**.

lizard a reptile with four short legs and a long tail. **Lizards** have skin like a snake.

llama a large South American animal with a long neck and woolly hair. **Llamas** look like small camels.

load things to be moved or carried. We put a **load** of hay in the stable.

loaf bread baked in a special shape. Sometimes **loaves** are sliced and sold in plastic bags.

lobster a shellfish with eight legs, two large claws and a tail.

lock a fastening for a door. You need a key to open a **lock**.

locomotive an engine on wheels that pulls carriages and wagons along railway lines.

log **1** a thick round length of wood. You can burn **logs** on a fire.
2 the diary of a ship's captain.

log-cabin a small house built mainly of logs.

lollipop a hard sweet made of boiled sugar on a stick.

lonely **1** having no friends.
2 feeling sad because you are alone.

long a great distance from one end to the other. We live a **long** way from the centre of town.

look-out someone who keeps watch.

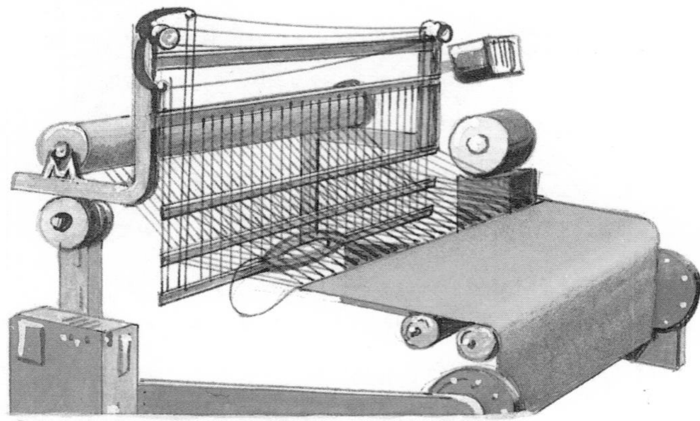

loom a machine used to weave thread into cloth.

loose 1 not tight. Carol often wears a **loose** shirt.
2 not fixed. One of my front teeth is **loose**.

lord a nobleman or ruler.

lose 1 to be unable to find something.
2 to fail to win a game or race.

lot very much or many. I like her a **lot**.

loud noisy.

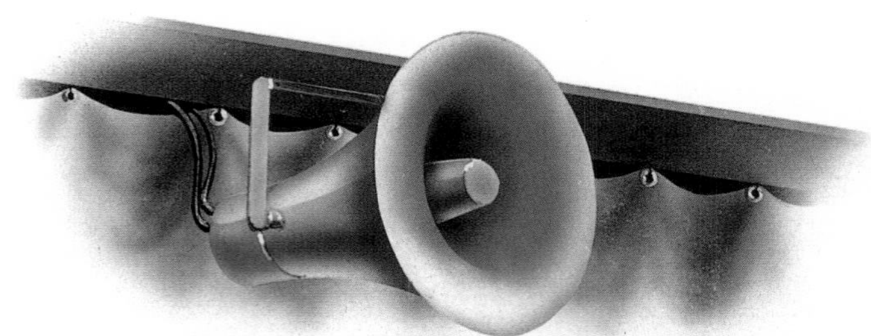

loud speaker an instrument that makes sounds louder.

love to like very much indeed.

low not high.

lucky having good fortune. Ted was **lucky** not to fall off his bicycle.

lumberjack someone who cuts down trees.

lunch the meal you have in the middle of the day.

lung one of the two parts inside your body used for breathing.

lynx a wild animal of the cat family. The **lynx** has a short tail and tufts on its ears.

machine something with moving parts which helps people to do their work. (See page 78)

mackerel a sea fish that you can eat.

magazine a kind of book or newspaper that comes out every week or month. **Magazines** are usually full of stories and colour pictures.

magic wonderful or mysterious things that cannot be easily explained. Witches and wizards cast **magic** spells.

magician someone who seems to make magical things happen.

magnet a piece of iron that can pull other bits of iron towards it.

magnificent wonderful to look at. The queen wore a **magnificent** jewelled crown.

magnifying glass a piece of glass that makes something look bigger than it really is.

magpie a black and white bird with a long tail. (See *birds* – page 19)

maid a woman servant.

mail letters, postcards and parcels you send through the post. Our **mail** is delivered twice a day.

main the most important. The **main** road runs through the centre of town.

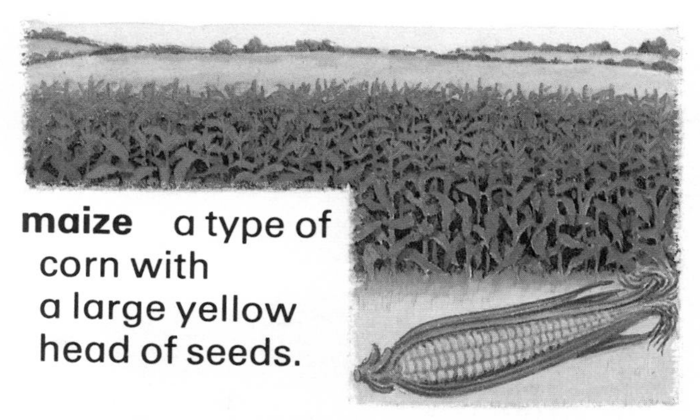

maize a type of corn with a large yellow head of seeds.

major **1** an officer in an army.
2 important.

make **1** to put something together or to build something. My baby sister **made** a tower from her building blocks.
2 to get someone to do something. The doctor **made** Jenny stay in bed for a day.

make-up things like powder and eye shadow you put on your face to make it look prettier.

machines

robot

digger

cement mixer

lawnmower

tractor

crane

male a person or animal that can become a father.

mallet a hammer with a wooden head.

malt a grain like barley which is used in making some food and drinks.

mammal one of a group of animals that can feed its babies with its own milk.

mammoth a huge creature of long ago that looked like an elephant covered with hair.

man a boy who has grown up.

manager someone who is in charge in an office, shop or factory.

mane the long hair on the neck of some animals. Lions and horses have **manes**.

manger a long open box that horses and cattle feed from in their stable.

mansion a very big house.

many a lot or a large number.

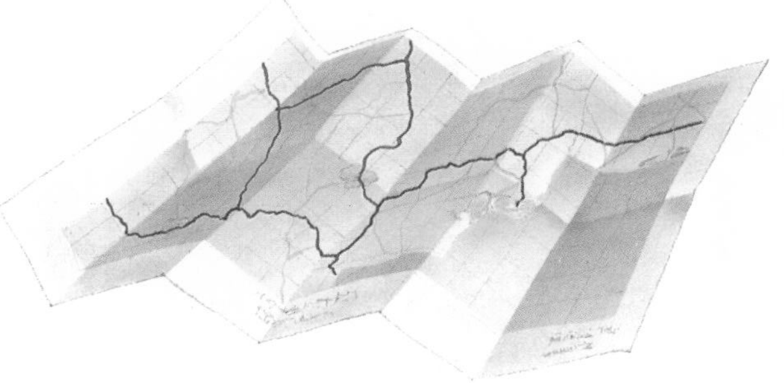

map a drawing to show where different places are in a city, a district or a country.

marbles a game played with little balls of coloured glass.

march to walk in step, like soldiers.

mare a female horse.

margarine a food that looks like butter and is made from vegetable oil.

marigold a bright orange or yellow flower like a daisy.

Mm

mark **1** a spot or line on something.
2 to point out something with a **mark.** The place where the treasure is buried is **marked** with a cross on the map.

market a place with stalls where people buy and sell things.

marmalade a kind of jam made from oranges or lemons.

marriage the joining of a man and a woman as husband and wife.

marsh soft, wet ground.

marzipan a sweet food made from almonds.

mascot an animal or object kept to bring good luck. The sports team carried a teddy bear as their **mascot**.

mask a covering for your face with holes for your eyes and mouth.

master a man in charge of people or things.

matador a man who fights bulls in Spain.

match
1 a small stick of wood with a special tip that makes fire when you strike it.
2 a competition between people or teams.
3 to be like something else in colour. My blue shoes and gloves are a perfect **match**.

mathematics the study of numbers, shapes and measurements.

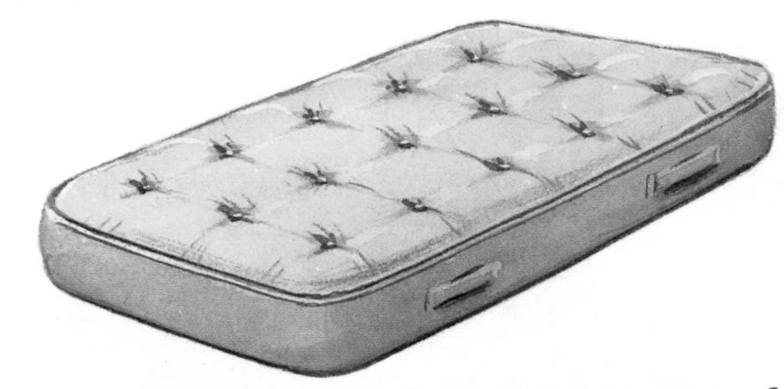

mattress the thick padded part of your bed that you sleep on.

mayor the chief person in a town or city.

maze a place with a lot of different paths to choose from. You have to choose the right path in the **maze** to find the way out.

meadow a field of grass for cattle or sheep to graze in.

meal the food we eat at one sitting. Breakfast, lunch and dinner are all **meals**.

measles an illness that makes your skin come out in red spots.

measure to find out how big or how long something is.

meat the flesh of animals used for food. Beef and chicken are **meat**.

mechanic someone who makes or mends machines.

medal a flat piece of metal on a ribbon that is given to someone as a reward for being brave or good at something.

medicine a drink or a tablet you take to make you better when you are not well.

meeting a group of people discussing something or listening to someone talking.

melon a large round juicy fruit with green or yellow skin. **Melons** have lots of seeds in the middle.

melt to heat something until it goes soft.

memory the ability to keep information in your mind. Lucy has a good **memory**; she can remember her third birthday party.

mend to repair something.

menu a list of things you can have for a meal in a restaurant or a café.

merchant someone who buys and sells goods.

Mm

meringue (sounds like merang) a sweet crumbly cake made from egg white and sugar.

mermaid a young and beautiful woman in fairy tales who lives in the sea and has the tail of a fish instead of legs.

merry cheerful.

merry-go-round a big machine at a fair where children sit and ride round on wooden animals.

mess an untidy jumble of things. Billy's toy cupboard was in a terrible **mess**.

message a piece of information you tell someone or send to them by letter. My father gave me a **message** for the teacher.

messenger someone who carries a message.

metal a hard material used to make things like ships, aeroplanes and cars.

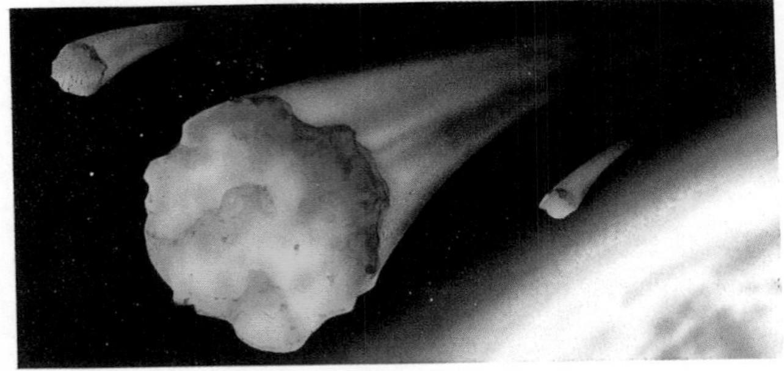

meteor a piece of rock or metal flying through space that burns up as it comes closer to the earth.

metre a measurement of length. There are 100 centimetres in one **metre**.

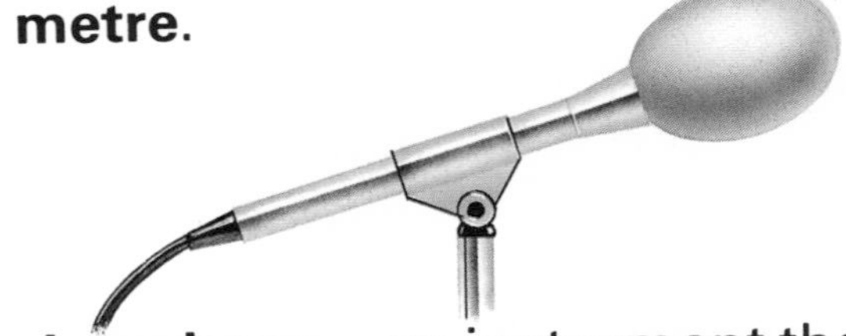

microphone an instrument that makes sounds, like talking or music, louder.

microscope an instrument you look through that makes small things look much bigger.

microwave a kind of electric wave used to heat foods quickly.

midday twelve o'clock in the day.

middle the centre part of something. There are white lines along the **middle** of the road.

midnight twelve o'clock at night.

midwife a nurse who helps women give birth.

mile a measurement of distance. A **mile** is equal to 1600 metres.

milk the white liquid made by human and animal females for feeding their babies. Cow's **milk** is a popular drink.

Milky Way the big white cloudy band of stars you can see across the sky at night.

mill 1 a building where corn is ground to make flour.
2 a factory where cloth or steel is made.

millimetre a measurement of length. There are 1000 millimetres in one **metre**.

millionaire someone who has one million pounds or one million dollars.

mince pie a sweet pie containing mincemeat.

mind 1 the power to think.
2 to be careful. **Mind** how you cross the road.

mine 1 belonging to me. This book is **mine**.
2 a deep hole in the ground where coal or metals are dug out.
3 a kind of bomb hidden under the earth or in the water.

miner someone who works in a coal or metal mine.

mineral useful rock that is dug out of the ground, like coal or diamonds.

minibus a small bus with seats for about 12 people.

minstrel a man who sang or played music in olden times.

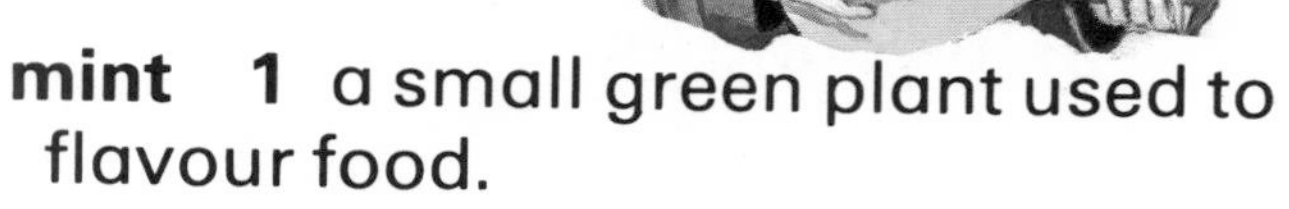

mint 1 a small green plant used to flavour food.
2 a sweet with the flavour of **mint**.
3 a building where money is made.

minus take away. 5 **minus** 4 leaves 1. In mathematics the sign for **minus** is –.

minute 1 (sounds like minnit) a measurement of time. There are 60 seconds in a **minute**.
2 (sounds like mynewt) very small indeed.

miracle a wonderful event that cannot be explained.

mirage a trick of the light that makes something appear that is not really there.

mirror a piece of glass you can see yourself in.

mischievous doing naughty or silly things.

miserable very unhappy.

miss 1 to be sad when someone is away. We **missed** our parents when they were abroad.
2 to fail to catch, hit or see something. Jane **missed** the ball when David threw it to her.
3 a young lady.

missile an explosive weapon fired against an enemy.

mistake something that has been done wrong. Bob made several **mistakes** in the spelling test.

mistletoe a green plant with small white berries. You can kiss someone under **mistletoe** at Christmas.

mittens a pair of gloves without separate places for your fingers.

mixture different things mixed together.

moat a deep ditch around a castle or a large house.

model 1 a small copy of something.
2 someone whose job is to wear new clothes to show people what they look like.

modern up to date.

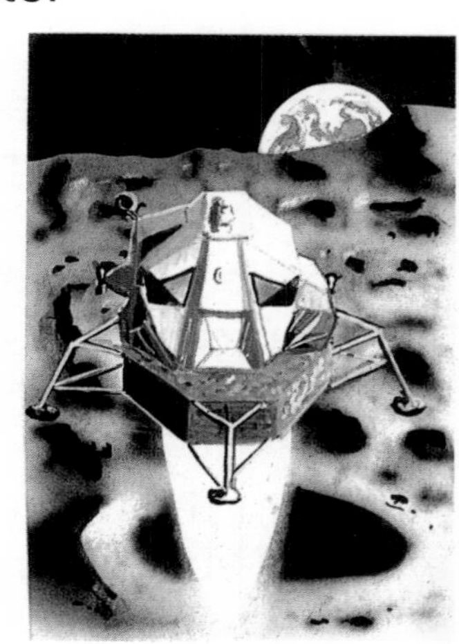

module part of a spacecraft that can be used separately from other parts. Spacemen can travel down to the moon's surface in a lunar **module**.

mole a small furry animal that digs tunnels and lives underground.

moment a very short time. We waited a **moment** before crossing the road.

monastery a set of buildings where monks live and work.

money coins or paper notes used for buying things.

mongrel a dog of mixed breeds.

monk a man who lives with a group of men who have taken religious vows.

monkey a furry animal with hands, feet and a tail. **Monkeys** are good at climbing trees. (See *animals* – page 11)

monsoon a season of heavy rain in some countries.

monster a big and terrifying animal in fairy stories.

month one of the twelve parts of the year. January is the first **month** of the year.

moon the bright planet we can see in the sky at night. The **moon** travels round the earth.

moonlight the light of the moon at night.

moor 1 a large area of rough land with few trees. I went riding on my pony across the **moor**.
2 to tie up a boat at the river's edge to stop it moving.

moose a large animal like a deer that lives in North America. The **moose** has large antlers.

mop a sponge or bundle of thick string on a long handle that you use for washing the floor.

more a greater number. There are **more** houses in our road than in the next road.

morning the time between sunrise and midday.

morse code a system of dots and dashes that mean letters of the alphabet. You can send messages by radio or flashing light using **morse code**.

mosaic a picture made from small coloured pieces of paper, glass or stone.

mosque a building in which Muslims worship.

mosquito a small flying insect that can bite you.

moss a small spongy plant that grows on damp stones or trees.

moth an insect like a butterfly. **Moths** usually fly about at night time.

mother a woman who has a child or children.

motor a machine that makes something move or work. The hairdrier stopped working because the **motor** burned out.

motorcycle a bicycle with an engine.

motorway a long wide straight road. Cars and trucks can travel fast for long distances on **motorways**.

mountain a very high hill.

mouse a small furry animal with a long tail and sharp teeth. (See *animals* – page 11)

moustache hair that grows above a man's top lip.

mouth **1** the opening in your face used for eating and speaking.
2 the place where a river meets the sea.

mouth organ a small musical instrument played by blowing through it.

move 1 to travel from one place to another.
2 to take something from one place to another.

movie a film you see at the cinema or on television.

muddle an untidy mess. All my toys are in a **muddle**.

mug a large cup with straight sides used without a saucer.

mule an animal which is half horse and half donkey.

multiply to make something a number of times bigger. Four **multiplied** by three is twelve.

multi-storey a building with many floors. We put our car in a **multi-storey** car park.

mummy 1 a child's name for mother.
2 a dead body that has been preserved. **Mummies** are sometimes discovered in ancient Egyptian tombs.

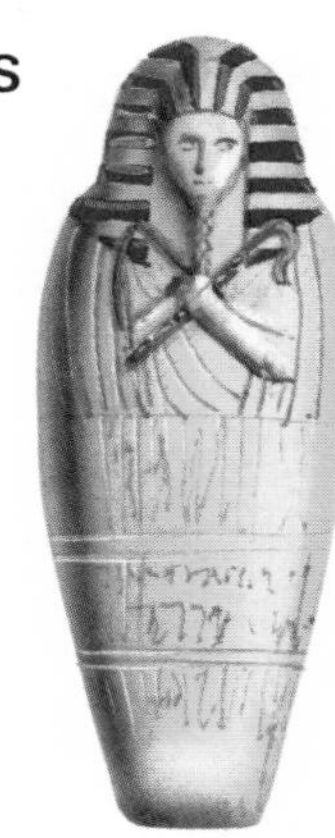

muscle one of the parts of the body that tighten and loosen to help you move.

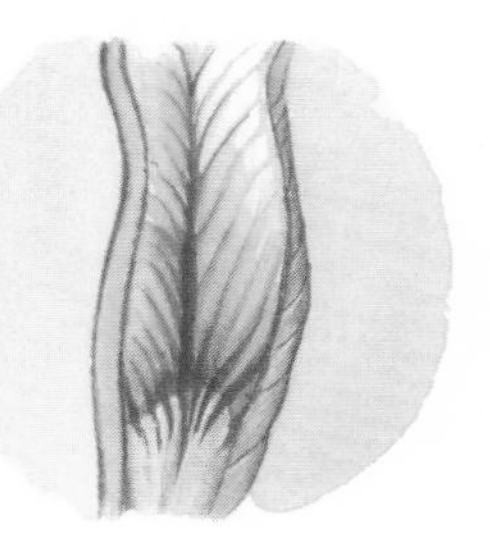

museum a place you can visit to see interesting things.

mushroom a plant that grows wild in fields and woods. **Mushrooms** look like small umbrellas.

music sounds made by singing or by playing an instrument.

musician a person who can play a musical instrument.

mussel a little sea creature that lives inside a black shell.

mustard a hot-tasting yellow paste you can use to flavour meat.

mystery something you cannot fully understand or explain.

myth a story that was made up long ago.

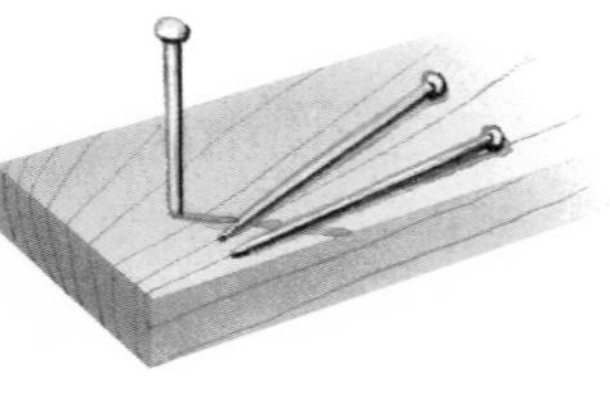

nail **1** a thin piece of metal with a point. You can hammer **nails** into wood.
2 the hard curved piece at the end of your fingers and toes.

name what someone or something is called. My cat's **name** is Tigger.

narrow thin; not wide. The path was so **narrow** we had to walk one behind the other.

nasty not nice; unpleasant.

native someone who is born in a certain land. Maria is a **native** of Mexico.

Nativity the birth of Jesus Christ.

nature **1** everything in the world that has not been made by people.
2 what someone is really like. Kelly has a generous **nature**.

naughty doing something that you are not supposed to do.

navigator someone who works out the right way to go in a ship, plane or a car.

navy the warships of a country and the people who sail in them.

near close to; not far away. We live **near** the church.

neat tidy and clean.

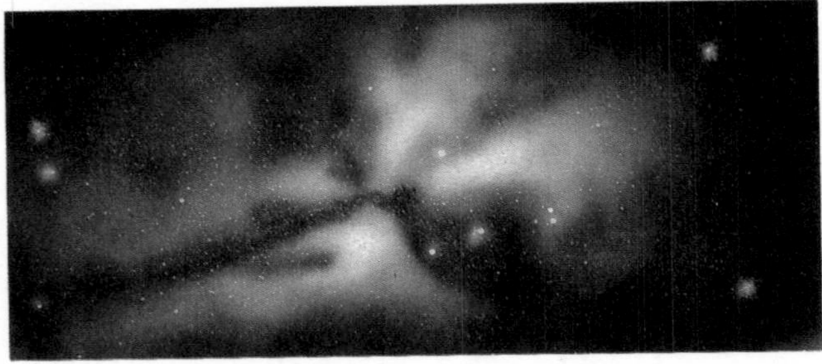

nebula a group of stars in a mass of gas way out in space.

necessary something that must be done. It was **necessary** for the doctor to come to the house.

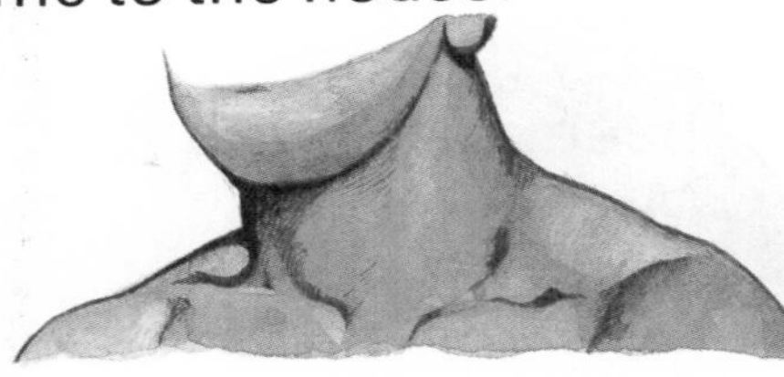

neck the part of the body between the head and the shoulders.

necklace a piece of jewellery you wear around your neck.

need to want something because you cannot do without it.

needle a thin piece of metal with a narrow hole at one end and a sharp point at the other. You use a **needle** for sewing.

needlework any work done on material using a needle and thread.

neighbour someone who lives near you. We asked our **neighbours** to come over on Sunday.

nephew the son of your brother or sister.

nervous worried or easily frightened. I am always **nervous** when I have to speak in front of the class.

nest a bird's home.

net lengths of string knotted together to make a material with holes in. Fishing **nets** are used to catch fish. **Nets** are also used in ball games like tennis and basketball.

nettle a wild plant with leaves that sting when you touch them.

never at no time. Sue **never** gets to school on time.

news written or spoken words about something that has just happened.

newspaper sheets of paper printed every day into a kind of book with news and pictures.

newt a very small animal like a lizard that lives in and out of the water.

next the nearest or the one after. My friend Jim lives in the **next** street.

nib the metal writing point of a pen.

nibble to eat food only a little bit at a time.

nickname a name your family or friends give you that is not your real name. My brother John was **nicknamed** Ginger because of his red hair.

niece the daughter of your brother or sister.

night the time between evening and early morning, when it is dark.

nightdress a dress worn in bed by women and girls.

nightingale a small brown bird famous for its singing voice.

nightmare a frightening dream that upsets you when you wake up.

nobody no person. **Nobody** went swimming because the water was too cold.

nocturnal being awake at night and sleeping in the daytime. Owls and bats are **nocturnal** animals.

noise a loud sound.

none not any. **None** of the shoes I had last year fits me now.

nonsense things that do not mean anything.

noon twelve o'clock in the day.

noose a loop in a piece of rope or string which can be made tight by pulling one end.

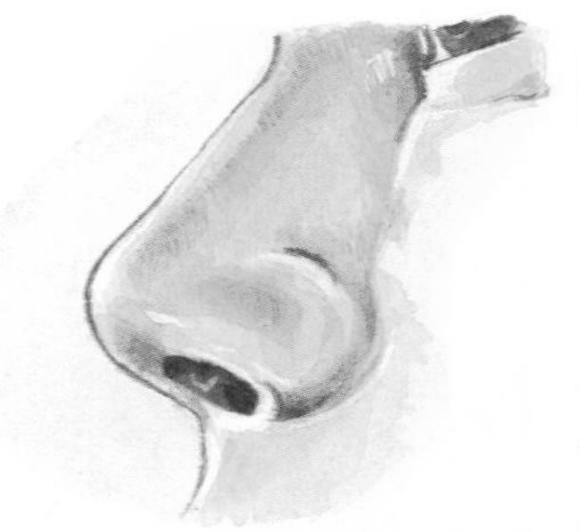

nose part of your face which you use for breathing in air and for smelling with.

nostril one of the two openings in your nose.

Nn

note 1 a short letter.
2 a piece of paper money.
3 a sound in music.

notebook a little book with blank paper which you can write in.

nothing not anything. There's **nothing** in that box; we emptied it this morning.

notice board a board fixed to a wall for messages.

nowhere not anywhere; in no place. Where did you go today? **Nowhere**, I stayed at home.

nozzle a piece on the end of a pipe or hose.

nuclear energy a form of power.

nuisance someone or something that annoys you or causes trouble.

numb not able to feel anything.

number a word or sign saying how many. Nine is a **number** that can also be written as 9.

nun a woman living with a group of women who have taken religious vows.

nurse someone who looks after people who are not well.

nursery 1 a school for very young children.
2 a place where plants are grown for sale.

nut the fruit or seed of a tree. Some **nuts** have hard shells.

nut-crackers a tool for cracking nutshells.

nylon a strong material used to make thread and clothes.

oak a tree that has seeds called acorns.

oar a wooden pole with a flat end. You use **oars** to row a boat.

oasis a place with water and trees in the middle of the desert.

obey to do as you are told.

oblong a four-sided shape like a door or a book.

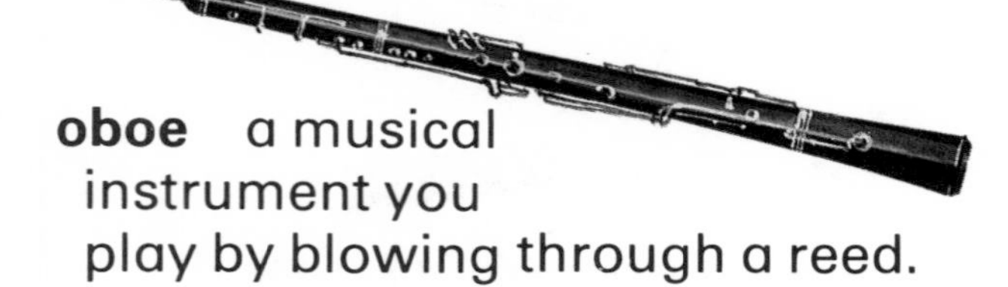

oboe a musical instrument you play by blowing through a reed.

observatory a special building for looking at the stars at night through a powerful telescope.

obstacle something that is in the way.

ocean a very large sea.

o'clock the time given on a clock. It is twelve **o'clock** when both hands of the clock point to the number 12.

octopus a sea creature with eight legs.

odd 1 unusual.
2 any number that is not even. 1, 3, 5 and 7 are all **odd** numbers.

office a room where people work at desks.

often many times. I **often** wake up early in the morning.

ogre a giant in fairy tales who eats people.

oil a thick liquid that makes engines run smoothly. **Oil** is also burned to heat and light buildings.

oil rig a platform for drawing up oil from the ground under the sea.

old 1 not new.
2 having lived a long time.

Olympics the Olympic Games. The **Olympics** is a great international sports event that is held every four years.

omelette food made from eggs mixed together and fried.

onion a round vegetable with a strong taste and smell. **Onions** grow under the ground.

only 1 no more than. Billy is **only** two years old.
2 one by itself. This apple was the **only** one left on the tree.

opera a musical play in which the actors and actresses sing the words.

opposite 1 as different as can be. Fat is the **opposite** of thin.
2 facing. We live **opposite** the school.

orange 1 a round juicy fruit with a thick skin.
2 the colour of an **orange**.

orbit the path of an object that moves around another object in space. The earth is in **orbit** around the sun.

orchard a field of fruit trees.

orchestra a group of musicians who play together.

order 1 things being kept in a particular place. The books in the library are kept in alphabetical **order**.
2 to tell someone to do something. We were **ordered** to sit down and keep quiet.

organ 1 a musical instrument with pipes, pedals and keys you play like a piano.
2 a part of the body. The heart and lungs are **organs**.

orphan a child whose parents are not alive.

Oo

ostrich a very large bird with long legs. **Ostriches** can run fast but they cannot fly.

other not this one. I found one of your ear-rings but I cannot find the **other** one.

otter a brown furry animal with a long tail and webbed feet. **Otters** live in or near water and eat fish.

ought should. He **ought** to clean his shoes before going to church.

outdoors in the open air. It is fun to be **outdoors** on a fine day.

outlaw someone in olden times who lived outside the law of the land. Jesse James was an **outlaw**.

oval egg-shaped.

oven part of a cooker that is like a metal cupboard. Food is baked in an **oven**.

overalls a kind of suit you wear over your clothes to keep them clean.

overseas abroad. My uncle Sam lives **overseas** in Africa.

overtake to catch up and then pass. Cars always **overtake** me when I ride my bicycle.

owl a night bird that has large eyes. **Owls** have a call that sounds like 'who-who'.

own to have something. Jason **owns** three dogs.

ox a big animal like a cow used for pulling a cart or plough.

oxygen one of the gases in the air we all breathe.

oyster a shellfish you can eat.

package a small parcel.

paddle **1** a long stick with a wide flat end. You use a **paddle** to move a canoe along the water.
2 to walk in shallow water in bare feet.

page one side of a sheet of paper in a book.

pagoda a Chinese temple that has many floors.

pail a bucket.

painful something that hurts you. The bruise on my knee is very **painful**.

paint
1 a coloured liquid that is put on with a brush.
2 to draw a picture using **paint** and brushes.

painting a picture that has been painted.

pair two things that are alike. I have a new **pair** of gloves.

palace a large building where a king or a queen lives.

pale without much colour; not looking well. David's face went **pale** when he saw the ghost.

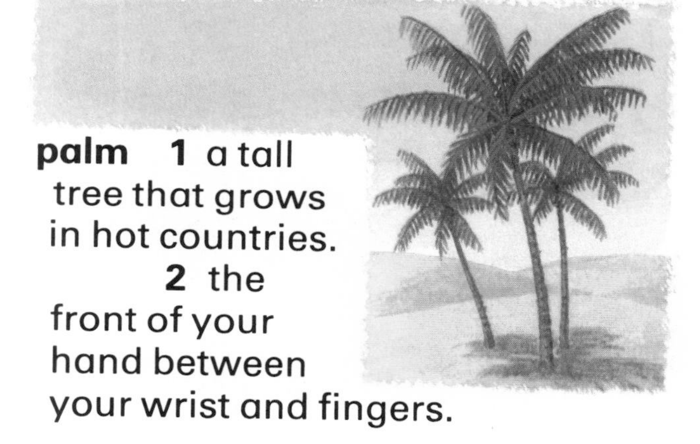

palm **1** a tall tree that grows in hot countries.
2 the front of your hand between your wrist and fingers.

pancake a flat round cake you make with milk, flour and eggs.

panda a large black and white animal that looks like a bear.

pane a piece of glass you put in a window frame.

pansy a small flower with brightly coloured petals.

Pp

panther a large wild cat like a leopard.

pantomime a musical play about a fairy tale.

paper the material that is used for writing or printing on, or for wrapping up parcels.

paperback a book that has a soft cover.

parachute a big sheet of strong silk with strings round the edge. If you jump from an aeroplane with a **parachute**, it opens up like an umbrella and lets you float gently down to the ground.

parade a line of people marching along.

parcel something wrapped up in paper. The postman brought me a **parcel** this morning.

parent a father or a mother.

park **1** a large open space with trees and grass where you can play.
2 to leave your car somewhere.

parrot a brightly coloured bird. Some **parrots** learn to talk.

part a piece of something.

pass **1** to move ahead of someone in front of you.
2 to hand something to someone else. Will you **pass** the salt please?
3 to get through a test.

passenger someone who travels in a vehicle, but who is not driving.

passport a special paper that you need to travel to other countries.

past **1** up to and beyond. The bus goes **past** our house.
2 the time that has gone. My grandfather likes to talk about the **past**.

pastry the crust around a pie or tart.

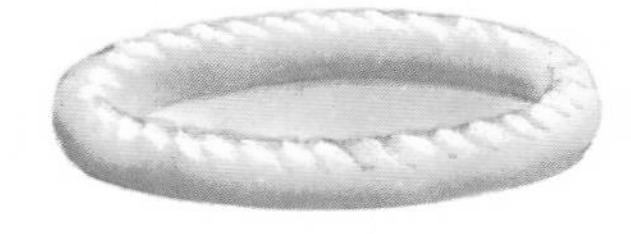

patch a small piece of cloth you put over holes in your clothes to mend them.

path a narrow lane you can walk or cycle along. There is a **path** from our house to the river.

patient 1 able to wait for something without getting annoyed.
2 someone who is looked after by a doctor.

pattern 1 something that you can use to copy a shape. Tailors cut out clothes from paper **patterns**.
2 a mixture of lines and shapes to make things like carpets and wallpaper look pretty.

paw an animal's foot.

pay 1 to give money for something you want.
2 money given to you for work you do.

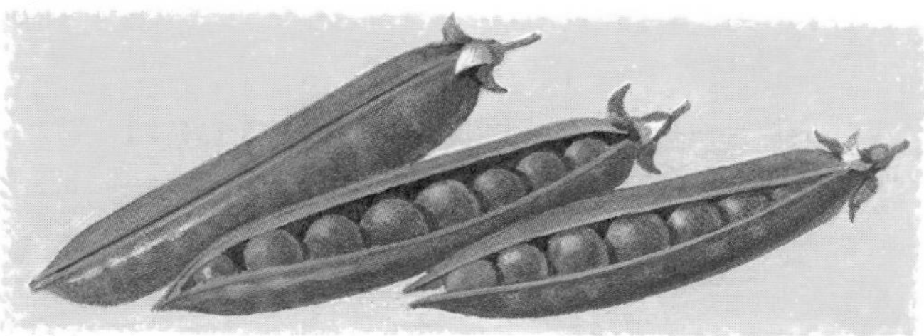

pea a small round green vegetable that grows in a pod.

peace 1 quiet.
2 the time when people are not at war.

peach a soft juicy red or yellow fruit with a stone in the middle.

peacock a large bird with a colourful tail shaped like a fan.

peanut a kind of nut that grows underground.

pear a juicy fruit with a yellow or green skin.

pearl a jewel found in some oyster shells.

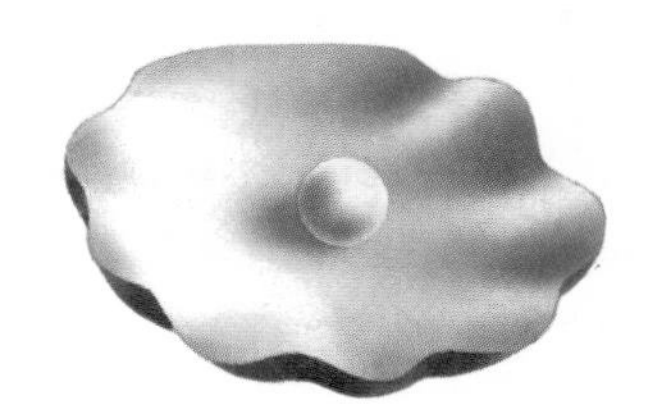

pebble a small round stone.

pedal a part of some machines that is worked by using your feet. Bicycles and cars have **pedals**.

pedestrian someone who is walking.

peel **1** the skin of fruits and vegetables.
2 to take off the skin of fruit or vegetables.

peg **1** a wooden or plastic clip that holds clothes on a line when they are drying.
2 a stick in the ground that you tie ropes around to hold up a tent.

pelican a water bird with a large pouch under its beak. **Pelicans** like to eat fish.

pencil a thin piece of wood with lead inside. You use a **pencil** to write or draw with.

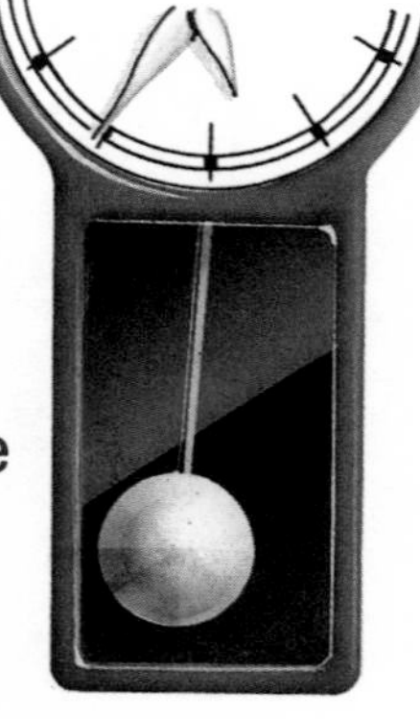

pendulum a weight that swings from side to side. Some clocks have a **pendulum** to make them keep time.

penguin a bird from the Antarctic with short legs and webbed feet. **Penguins** can swim but they cannot fly. (See *birds* – page 19)

penicillin a kind of medicine.

penknife a small knife. The blade of a **penknife** folds into its handle.

penny a coin of small value.

people men, women, boys and girls.

pepper **1** a red, green or yellow vegetable used in cooking and in salads.
2 black or white powder used to flavour food.

perfume a liquid with a pleasant smell. People put on **perfume** to make themselves smell nice.

periscope a tube with mirrors in it. **Periscopes** are used in submarines to see above the water.

petal one of the coloured parts of a flower.

petrol a liquid made from oil. **Petrol** is used in engines to make them work.

photograph a picture you take with a camera.

piano a large musical instrument with black and white keys you play with your hands.

piccolo a musical instrument like a small flute.

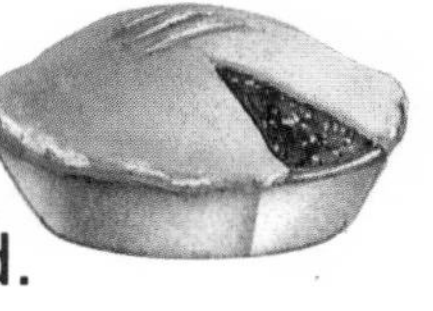

pick **1** to choose.
2 to gather.
3 a heavy tool used to break up earth.

picnic a meal eaten outdoors.

picture a drawing, painting or photograph.

pie a dish of fruit or meat covered with pastry and baked.

piece a bit of something. The jigsaw puzzle has 100 **pieces**.

pig a fat pink animal with a curly tail.

pigeon a grey bird that can be taught to find its way home from a long way away.
(See *birds* – page 19)

pigtail hair plaited to hang from your head down your back.

pile a heap.

pill a small ball of medicine that you can swallow to make you feel better when you are sick.

pillar a tall wooden or stone post that holds up a roof or floor above it.

pillow a cloth bag with soft material. You rest your head on a **pillow** while you sleep.

pilot **1** someone who flies an aeroplane.
2 someone who steers a ship into harbour.

pinch to squeeze something between your fingers and thumb.

pineapple a big yellow fruit with a thick skin.

pipe **1** a long tube that liquid or gas can run through.
2 a short tube with a bowl at one end for tobacco. Some people smoke **pipes**.

pirate someone in olden times who attacked ships at sea to rob them of their treasure.

pistol a small gun.

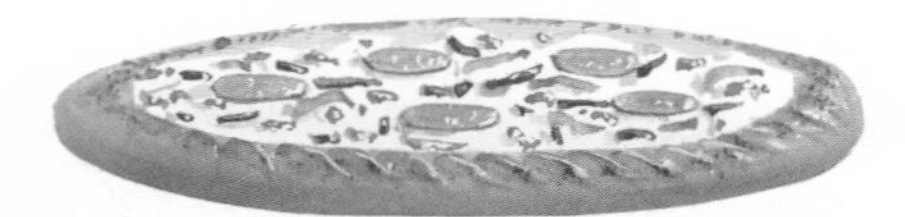

pizza an Italian food of cheese and tomatoes and other toppings on a flat base of dough.

planet one of the worlds in space that move around the sun. Mercury is the nearest **planet** to the sun.

plank a long flat piece of wood.

plant something that grows up from the ground, like a bush or a flower.

plaster **1** a sticky piece of material you put over a cut or sore.
2 a powder that you mix with water to make it hard. **Plaster** is used in building work and for putting around broken arms and legs.

plastic a tough, light material. **Plastic** is used to make many things.

plate a flat dish you put your food on.

platform the place where passengers stand at a railway station to go on a train.

play **1** to have a game.
2 a story which is acted on a stage.
3 to make music on an instrument.

playground the place where you play games at school.

Pp

plenty more than you need. There is **plenty** of food for the barbecue.

plough (rhymes with cow) a farm machine that digs over the soil.

plug **1** a stopper you put in the hole in a sink or a bath to stop water from running away.
2 a fitting that joins the wires from any electric machine to the main supply.

plum a soft juicy fruit with a large stone. **Plums** can be yellow, red or purple.

plumber someone who fits and mends taps and water pipes.

pocket a small bag sewn into your clothes. You can carry small things like money and a handkerchief in your **pockets**.

poem words written in verse.

poison a dangerous liquid or powder that can kill living things.

polar bear a large white bear that lives in the Arctic.

pole a long thick stick made of wood or metal.

police the people who make sure that we obey the law.

polish **1** to rub something to make it shine.
2 a paste or liquid you use to make things shine.

pond a small lake in a park or garden.

pool **1** a very small area of still water.
2 a place filled with water where you go for a swim.

poor without much money. He was too **poor** to buy some new gloves.

popcorn crunchy grains of corn that have been swollen by heating them. People often eat **popcorn** at the cinema.

Pp

poppy a bright red flower that grows wild.

porcupine an animal like a large hedgehog. **Porcupines** have short legs and long stiff prickles. (See *animals* – page 11)

porpoise a sea creature that looks like a small whale.

port **1** a town with docks and harbours.
2 a strong drink made from grapes.
3 the left side of a ship.

possible something that can be done. It is **possible** to run a mile in under four minutes.

post **1** to send letters, parcels and cards through the **post** office.
2 the letters, parcels and cards the **post**man delivers.
3 a pole sticking in the ground.

postcard a card you write on and send by post. Some **postcards** have colour pictures on one side.

poster a large colourful picture you can stick on your wall.

post office the place where you can buy stamps and post parcels.

potato a vegetable that grows underground. You can boil, bake or fry **potatoes**.

pottery cups, plates and ornaments made from clay.

pound **1** a sum of money. One **pound** is equal to 100 pence.
2 a measurement of weight. One **pound** weight is about half a kilogramme.

pour **1** to tip a liquid out of a bottle or jug.
2 to rain very hard.

power the strength or ability to do something.

prayer talking to God.

prehistoric in the time before history was written down. Dinosaurs are **prehistoric** animals.

present 1 something that is given.
2 the time now. My father is away at **present** but he comes home next week.
3 here. The teacher marked the whole class **present**.

president someone who is in charge of a country, a company or a club.

pretend to try to be something or someone you are not. Let's **pretend** to be doctors and nurses.

price how much money something costs to buy.

prince the son of a king or queen.

princess the daughter of a king or queen.

print to put words and pictures onto paper using a printing machine.

prison a building where criminals are kept.

private 1 not open to everyone. This is **private** property.
2 the lowest rank of soldier in an army.

prize a reward for winning something.

program instructions given to a computer for it to work out certain problems.

projector a machine for showing still or moving pictures on a screen.

promise to give your word that you will do something. I **promise** to make a cake for your birthday.

propellor blades that turn to drive an aeroplane or a ship.

prune a dried plum.

pudding a soft sweet food which you eat after your main course.

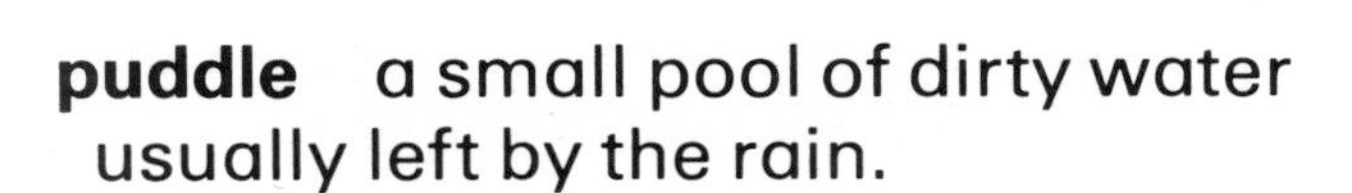

puddle a small pool of dirty water usually left by the rain.

Pp

puffin a sea bird with a short thick colourful beak.

pull to take hold of something and drag it towards you.

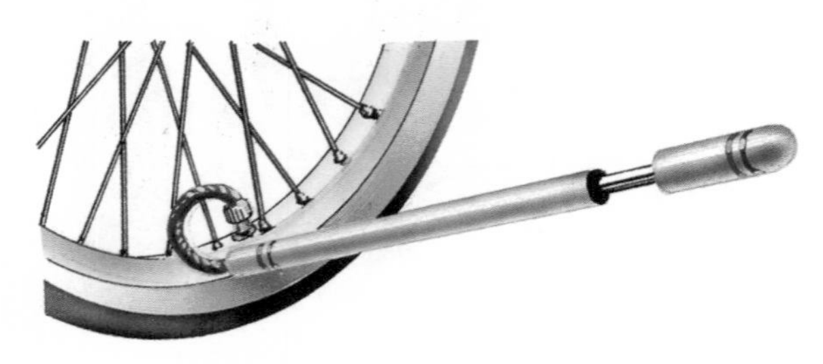

pump a machine that pushes liquids or air through a pipe. You **pump** air into bicycle tyres with a **pump**.

pumpkin a very large fruit with a hard yellow skin.

punchbag a stuffed bag that boxers use to practise their punching.

puncture a hole made in a tyre.

pupil **1** a child at school.
2 the black dot in the middle of your eye which you see through.

puppet a doll that you move by putting a hand inside it or by pulling it with strings.

purse a little bag you carry around with you to keep your money in.

push to move something away from you.

puzzle something that needs solving before you can find the answer.

pylon a metal tower that holds up electricity wires.

pyramid the buildings where Ancient Egyptians used to bury their dead kings. A **pyramid** has four triangular sides on a square base.

python a very large snake.

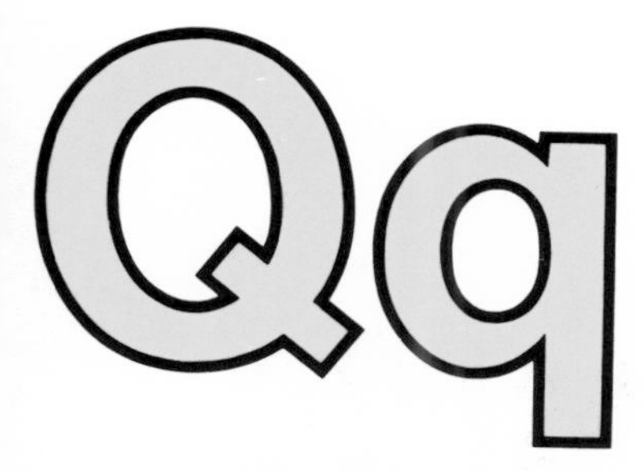

quack the sound a duck makes.

quantity how much or how many.

quarrel an argument where people get angry with each other.

quarry a place where stone or gravel is dug out of the ground.

quarter one of four equal parts of something. If you cut a cake into **quarters** you will have four equal pieces.

quay (sounds like key) the landing place in a harbour where boats or ships can be loaded and unloaded.

queen
1 a woman who rules a country.
2 a woman who is the wife of a king.

question something you ask when you want to know something.

queue (sounds like kew) people or vehicles waiting in a line. There was a **queue** of people outside the cinema.

quick able to do something in a very short time. He was **quick** at adding up numbers.

quiet making very little noise. Robert's voice is so **quiet** you can hardly hear him.

quill a long feather you can use as a pen.

quilt a warm padded covering for a bed.

quit to give up.

quite **1** completely. I was sick last week but now I'm **quite** better.
2 fairly. Chris is **quite** tall for her age.

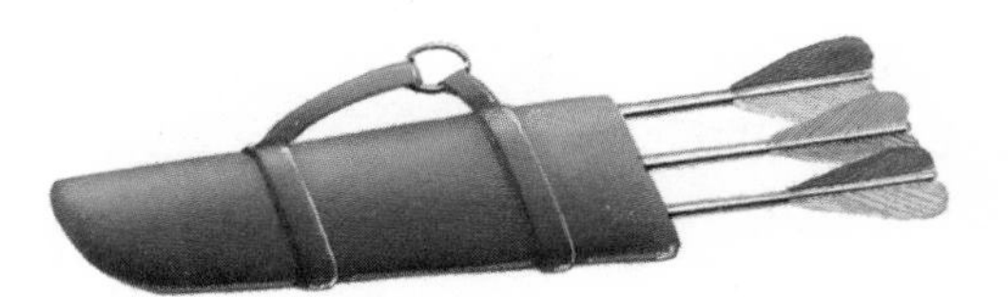

quiver **1** a leather case that holds arrows.
2 to tremble or to shake.

quiz a test of knowledge.

Rr

rabbit a little furry animal with long ears. **Rabbits** live underground. (See *animals* – page 11)

raccoon a small wild animal that has a long tail with black rings on it.

race **1** a running or swimming competition.
2 a group of people who come from the same part of the world.

racket a bat with strings in it. You use a **racket** to play tennis.

radar a way of spotting objects like ships and aircraft using radio waves.

radiator **1** a metal object which can be heated to warm a room.
2 a container in the front of a car that has water in it to cool the engine.

radio an instrument that sends or receives voices and music through the air.

radish a small red-skinned vegetable you eat raw.

raffle a competition in which many people buy tickets. Prizes are given to those holding a winning **raffle** ticket.

raft logs tied together to make a flat boat that floats on the water. We crossed the river on a **raft**.

rage great anger.

raid a surprise attack.

rail a large metal or wooden bar.

railing a fence made with metal rails.

railway the track that trains run on.

Rr

rain water that falls from clouds in drops.

rainbow a band of bright colours in the sky when the sun shines through the rain. There are seven colours in a **rainbow**.

raincoat a long coat you wear to keep dry when it rains.

raise **1** to lift up. **Raise** your hands above your head.
2 to collect the money needed for a particular purpose.

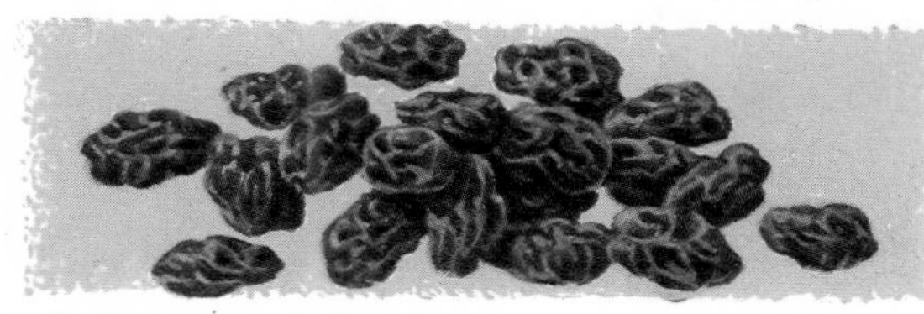

raisin a dried grape used in cakes and puddings.

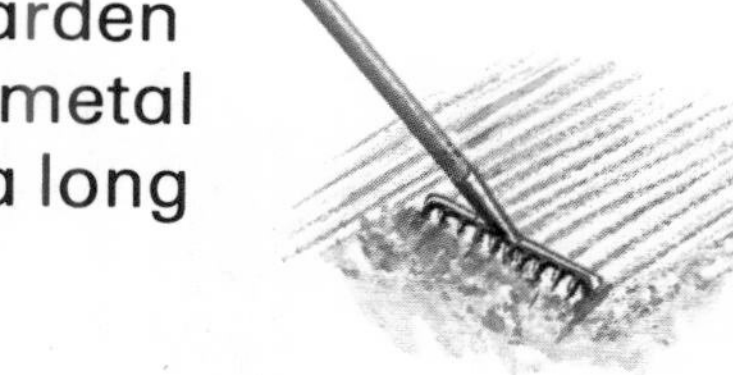

rake a garden tool with metal teeth on a long handle.

ram **1** a male sheep.
2 to push something very hard into something else.

ramble a long walk in the countryside.

ranch a large farm for cattle, horses or sheep.

range **1** the distance a missile, like a bullet or arrow, can travel.
2 a line of mountains.

raspberry a small soft red fruit with lots of seeds.

rat a small animal with long sharp teeth. A **rat** looks like a large mouse.

rattle **1** the sound of things shaking together.
2 a baby's toy that makes a rattling sound.

rattlesnake a poisonous snake that makes a rattling sound with its tail.

raven a large black bird with shiny feathers. (See *birds* – page 19)

raw not cooked.

ray a thin band of light.

razor a tool with a sharp blade for shaving hairs off your chin.

reach **1** to arrive somewhere.
2 to stretch out your hand to touch something.

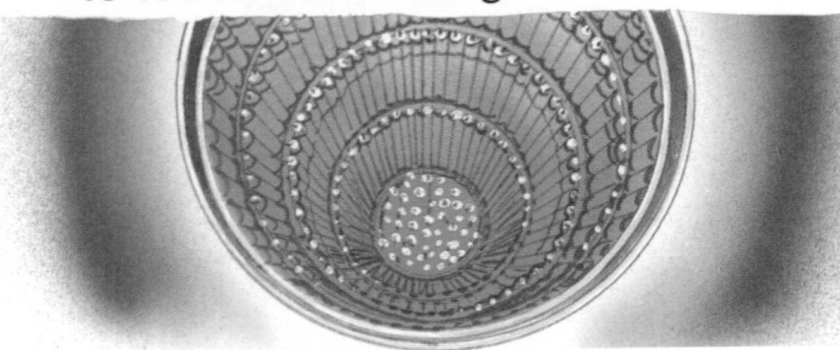

reactor a container where mixed chemicals work together to produce energy.

read to be able to say and understand words that are written down.

ready waiting to start something.

real not made up; not a copy. My mother has a **real** diamond ring.

reason the explanation of something that has happened. The **reason** he was late was that he missed the bus.

rebel **1** (sounds like rebble) someone who goes against his leader.
2 (sounds like re-bell) to go against your leader.

receive to take something given to you.

recipe (sounds like ressippee) a list of things you need and what to do with them to make a dish or a meal.

record **1** a disc you play on a record player.
2 the best performance in a competition.

recorder a wooden musical instrument you blow down to make music.

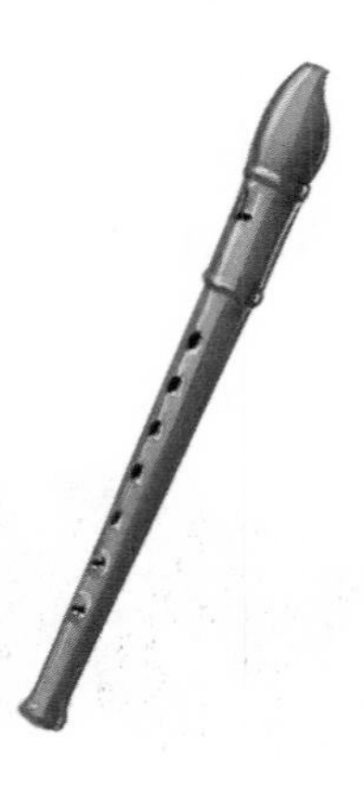

record player a machine for playing records.

rectangle a shape with four sides.

reed a tall kind of grass with a hollow stem. **Reeds** grow where there is water.

Rr

referee the person who makes sure players in a game follow the rules.

reflection the picture seen in a shiny surface. If you look in a mirror or still water you will see your own **reflection**.

refrigerator a kind of cupboard that keeps food and drinks cold.

refuse to say no when you are asked to do something.

register a list of people's names.

rehearsal (sounds like rehursal) a practice for a concert or a play.

reign the time a king or queen rules. The **reign** of Queen Victoria lasted 63 years.

reindeer a kind of deer that has very large horns. **Reindeer** live in cold countries.

reins the straps you use to guide a horse while you ride.

relation a member of your family.

remember to put something into your memory and not forget it.

remote control a system that makes a machine work from a distance using radio signals.

repair to mend.

reply to answer a question.

reporter someone who writes or talks about things that have just happened. **Reporters** work for newspapers, radio and television.

reptile a creature that has cold blood and scaly skin. Lizards, snakes and crocodiles are **reptiles**.

Rr

rescue to save someone from danger. The helicopter **rescued** the passengers from the sinking ship.

reservoir a place where drinking water is stored in huge pools.

rest 1 to stop working or playing and stay still.
2 the others. We kept one kitten and gave the **rest** away.

restaurant a place where you can buy and eat a meal.

result how something ends.

return 1 to come back.
2 to give back.

revolver a small hand gun.

reward a present or a prize for doing well in something.

rhinoceros a big wild animal with thick grey skin and a long curved horn on its head.

rhubarb a plant with thick red stalks you cook and eat.

rhyme word endings that sound the same. The words 'wool' and 'full' **rhyme**.

rhythm a steady beat of sounds in music or poetry.

rib one of the curved bones in your chest.

ribbon a thin piece of material you use to tie up your hair or to decorate your clothes.

rice a kind of grain grown in some hot countries. **Rice** is an important food in many lands.

rich having lots of money.

Rr

riddle a kind of puzzle in words which asks a question that is difficult to answer.

ride to travel in or on something that moves. You can **ride** a bicycle, a horse or in a car.

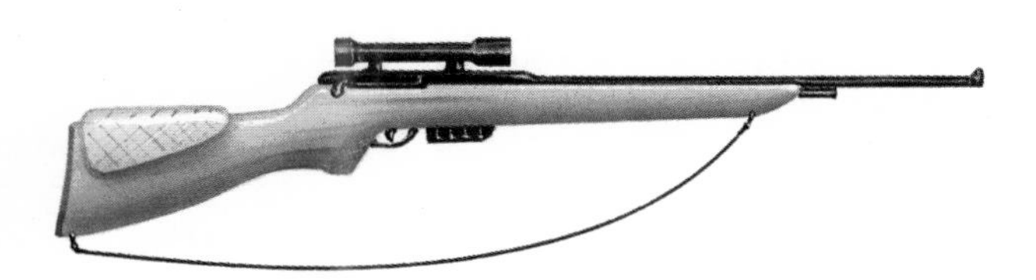

rifle a long gun that is held against the shoulder to shoot.

right 1 the opposite of left. In America we drive on the **right** side of the road.
2 correct. He gave the **right** answer.
3 good. It is not **right** to hurt other people.

ring 1 a circular band of silver or gold which you wear on your finger. Some **rings** have jewels in them.
2 a circle.
3 the sound made when you strike a bell.
4 to telephone someone.

rip to tear something apart. The gale **ripped** the garage roof off.

ripe when a fruit or vegetable is fully grown and ready to eat.

river a long stretch of water that flows over land into the sea or into a lake.

road a hard surface made for traffic to travel on from place to place.

roam to wander around.

roar a loud noise made by some large animals like lions and tigers.

roast to cook meat in an oven or over an open fire.

robbery the act of stealing.

robe a long gown that covers you right down to your ankles.

robin a small bird with red feathers at the front.

robot a machine that is able to do some of the things a person can do. (See *machines* – page 78)

Rr

rock **1** a large piece of stone.
2 to move gently from side to side.
3 a type of music.
4 a hard sweet shaped like a stick.

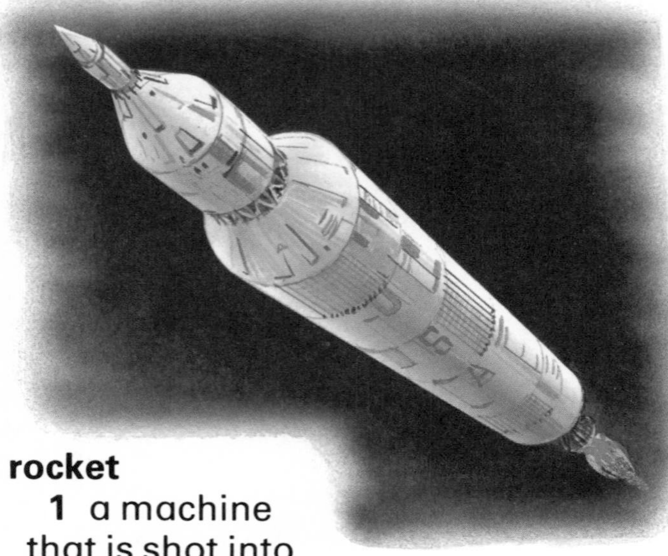

rocket
1 a machine that is shot into space.
2 a type of firework you send up into the air.

rocking chair an armchair that rocks backwards and forwards when you sit in it.

rocking horse a wooden horse that rocks backwards and forwards when you ride it.

rod a long thin bar of wood or metal.

rodeo an American show where cowboys show off their skills. They lasso cattle and ride wild horses at **rodeos**.

roll **1** to move along by turning over and over.
2 a small piece of bread baked in the shape of a ball.
3 something the shape of a tube like a **roll** of wallpaper.

roller skates special boots with wheels on.

roof the cover on the top of a building.

room **1** a space inside a building surrounded by walls. The kitchen is the **room** where food is cooked.
2 space to put things on. Is there any **room** for my books on the shelf?

root the part of a tree or plant that grows underground.

rope very thick string.

rose a sweet-smelling flower with thorny stems.

rotor blades the blades on the top of a helicopter that turn round fast and lift it into the air.

rough **1** not smooth or even.
2 wild and stormy. The sea was very **rough** because of the high winds.

roulette a game where a ball is thrown into a spinning wheel with numbered spaces. You have to guess which number the ball will land on when the wheel stops spinning.

round **1** the shape of a circle.
2 the length of time boxers fight in the ring before they can take a rest.

roundabout **1** a circular machine in a children's playground.
2 a circular island at a road junction.

rounders a game for two teams using a bat like a stick and a heavy ball.

row **1** (rhymes with go) a line of people or things.
2 to move a small boat in the water using oars.
3 (rhymes with cow) a noisy quarrel.

rowing-boat a small boat you row through the water.

royal describing something to do with a king or a queen. The prince and princess are members of the **royal** family.

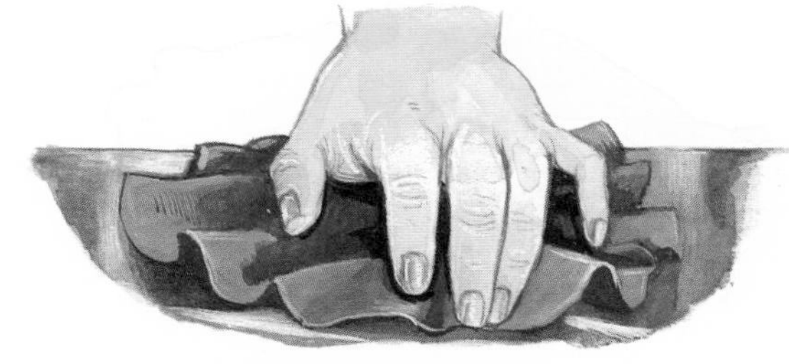

rub to wipe something hard with a cloth.

rubber **1** material from a rubber tree that stretches and bounces.
2 a lump of rubber you use to remove pencil marks from paper.

rubbish things you throw away because you do not want them.

ruby a bright red stone of great value. **Rubies** are used in jewellery.

rucksack a large bag you can carry on your back. People carry all their things in **rucksacks** when they go on walking trips.

Rr

rudder a piece of wood or metal on the back of a boat or aeroplane. You move the **rudder** to change direction.

rude not polite.

rug a small carpet.

rugby a game for two teams played with an oval ball. **Rugby** players can kick, pass or run with the ball to score points.

ruin **1** an old building that has fallen down.
2 to spoil.

ruler **1** an instrument that you use for measuring and drawing straight lines.
2 someone who is head of a country.

run to move fast on your feet.

rung one of the steps of a ladder.

runner bean a long thin green vegetable that grows on a climbing plant.

runway a long straight road on an airfield where aircraft take off and land.

rush **1** to hurry.
2 a tall grass that grows in or near water.

rush hour a time of day when cities become crowded by people travelling to and from work.

rust the brown marks you find on rotting metal.

rye a kind of grain you can make into flour for bread.

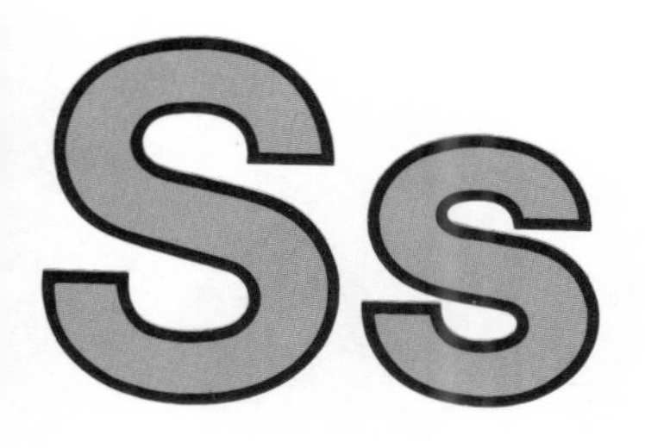

sack a large bag made from paper, plastic or rough cloth. **Sacks** are used for carrying or storing things.

saddle the leather seat on a bicycle or that you put on a horse.

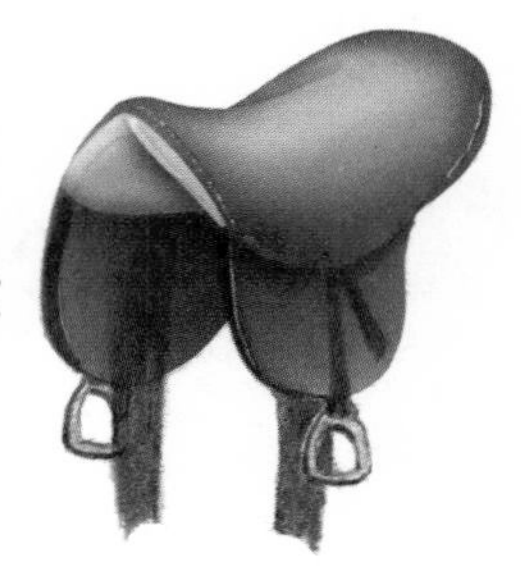

safari a journey in search of wild animals.

safe 1 out of danger. It is **safe** to cross the road when there is no traffic.
2 a strong box or cupboard where you keep money and jewellery locked away.

sailor someone who works as a member of the crew on a ship.

sale a time when goods are sold in shops at less than the normal price.

salmon a large fish with silvery skin.

salt a white powder used to flavour food.

same like someone or something else. John goes to the **same** sports club as my sister.

sandal a kind of open shoe with straps.

sandcastle a small castle you build out of sand when you are playing at the seaside.

sandwich two slices of bread and butter with a tasty filling in between.

satchel a bag for carrying school books in.

satellite 1 a planet that goes around a larger planet. The moon is a **satellite** of the earth.
2 an instrument that travels in space around the earth and sends signals. Some **satellites** send out television pictures.

sauce a thick liquid put on some foods to make them tastier.

saucepan a pan with a handle used for cooking.

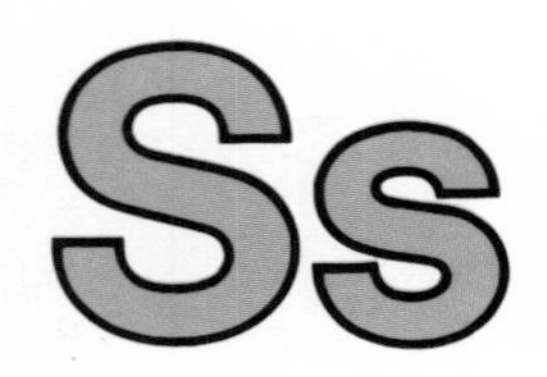

saucer the dish you put under a cup to catch the drips.

sausage a food made of minced meat and bread put into a thin skin and then cooked.

save **1** to help someone out of danger. The lifeguard **saved** the boy from drowning in the lake.
2 to keep something so that you can use it later. I **saved** one chocolate to have tomorrow.

savings money you put aside in a box or at the bank for later use.

saw a tool that has a flat blade with sharp teeth along one side. **Saws** are used for cutting wood.

saxophone a brass musical instrument you play by blowing.

scales a machine for weighing people or things.

scarecrow a model of a person dressed in old clothes. **Scarecrows** stand in a field to frighten birds away from seeds and crops.

scarf a long piece of cloth you wear around your neck.

scene **1** a view.
2 a part of a play.
3 the place where something happened.

school the place where you go to learn.

science the study of how things work and why things happen.

science fiction stories made up about the future.

scissors a cutting tool made from two blades that open and shut together.

scooter a toy with two wheels that you stand on with one foot and push with the other.

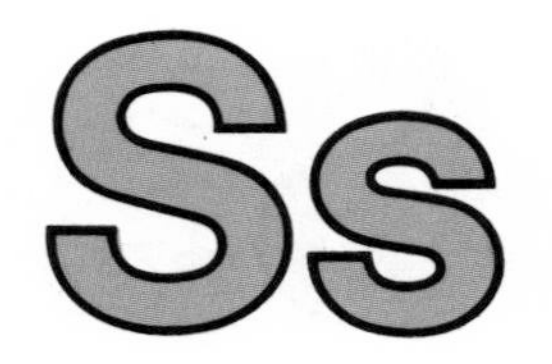

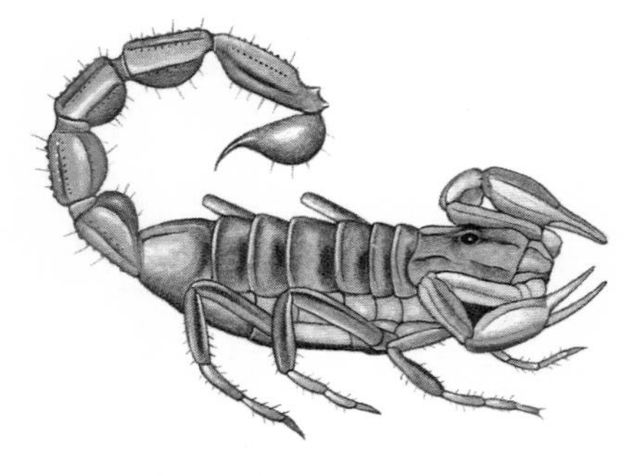

scorpion a creature belonging to the spider family. **Scorpions** have a poisonous sting in their tails.

scrape to clean or rub with something sharp like a knife.

scratch 1 a small cut on your skin.
2 to rub your skin to stop it itching.

scream a very loud cry.

screw a kind of nail with a groove at the top. You turn a **screw** round and round in a hole to hold something tightly in place.

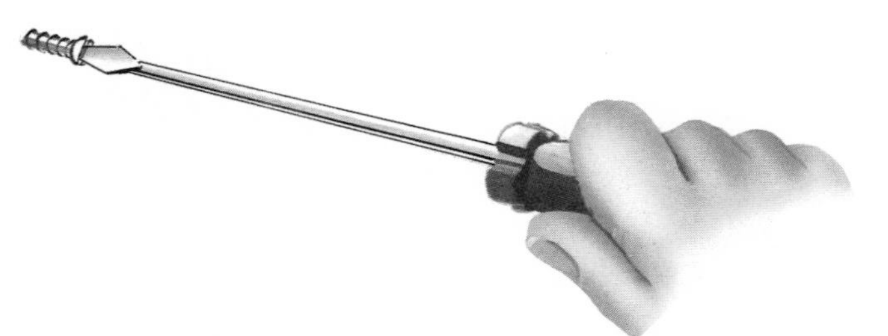

screwdriver a tool for turning a screw.

scribble to write quickly and untidily.

scrubbing brush
a stiff brush used for cleaning something with soap and water.

sea the salty water that covers most of the world.

seagull a white and grey sea bird that is often found at the seashore.

seahorse a small sea animal in the shape of a tiny horse.

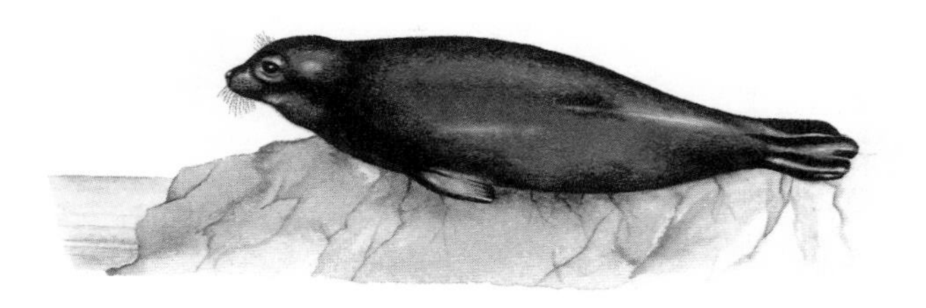

seal a soft furry animal with flippers. **Seals** can live on land and in the water.

search to look carefully. The detective **searched** the room for a clue.

seat belt a belt you put around you when you travel in a car. **Seat belts** hold you in your seat if the car stops suddenly.

seaweed
a type of wild plant that grows under the sea. **Seaweed** is often washed on to the beach.

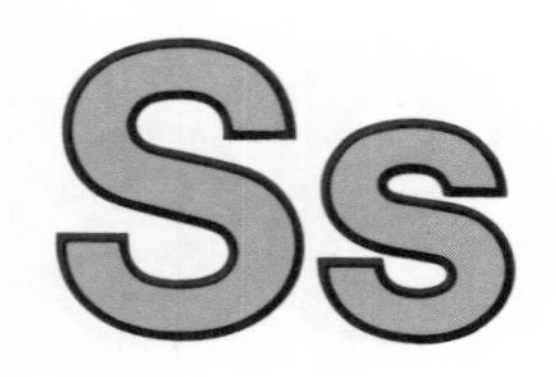

second 1 the one after the first. He came **second** in the race.
2 a very short time. There are 60 **seconds** in one minute.

secret something that is kept hidden from other people.

secretary someone who works for another person doing office work. **Secretaries** often type letters and answer the telephone.

seed the part of a plant that you put into the ground for a new plant to grow.

seek to look for.

see-saw a long piece of wood balanced at the middle. One person sits at either end making it go up and down.

send to make someone or something go somewhere. Did David **send** a birthday card to you?

serve 1 to help people. The assistant **serves** people in a shop.
2 to play the first shot in racket games like tennis.

settee a long soft seat for two or three people.

sewing machine a machine for sewing clothes very quickly.

shade 1 a cover for a light.
2 a place that is in shadow when the sun is out.

shadow the dark shape an object or a person makes when standing in front of a light or under the sun.

shake to move something up and down or side to side very quickly.

shampoo a soapy liquid for washing your hair.

share to give part of what is yours to someone else. Would you like to **share** my birthday cake?

shark a large and dangerous fish with very sharp teeth.

Ss

sharp pointed or able to cut easily. Jo's penknife has a **sharp** blade.

shave to cut hair from your face with a razor. Most men **shave** once a day.

shawl a piece of cloth or knitting you wear over your shoulders or wrap around a baby.

shears a garden tool like a large pair of scissors. You can cut long grass with garden **shears.**

shed a wooden hut in the garden or on a building site.

sheep a farm animal which we get wool from.

sheet **1** a large piece of material that is spread on a bed. **2** a piece of paper.

sheik an Arab prince or chief.

shelf a piece of wood or metal fixed to a wall. Books and ornaments can be kept on a **shelf.**

shell a hard covering. Nuts, eggs and some animals have **shells.**

shelter a place where you are safe from bad weather or from danger.

shepherd someone who looks after sheep.

sheriff an officer of the law in some countries. Wyatt Earp was a famous **sheriff** in the wild west.

shield a piece of metal or hard leather that you hold to protect your body. Knights in battle held a weapon in one hand and a **shield** in the other.

shine to give off a bright light. The street lamp **shines** on our gate.

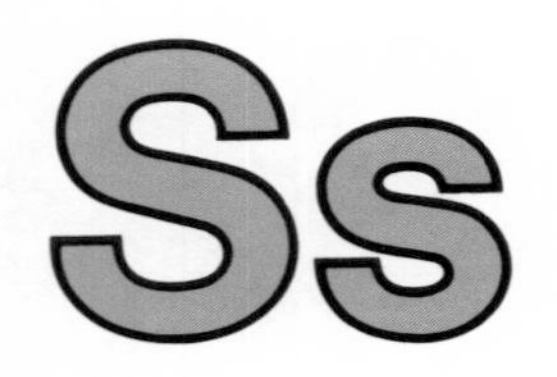

ship a large boat that travels across the sea.
(See *transport*—page 141)

shipwreck a ship that has sunk at sea.

shirt a piece of clothing that covers the top part of your body. **Shirts** usually have buttons down the front.

shiver to shake a lot when you are cold or when you are frightened.

shock a nasty surprise. Judy had a **shock** when she saw her bag was empty.

shoe what you wear on your feet. Some **shoes** have laces to do them up.

shoot to fire a bullet from a gun or an arrow from a bow.

shop a building where you buy things.

shore land along the water's edge.

shorts short trousers. Athletes wear **shorts** for running.

shoulder the joint between your body and your arm.

shout to speak loudly.

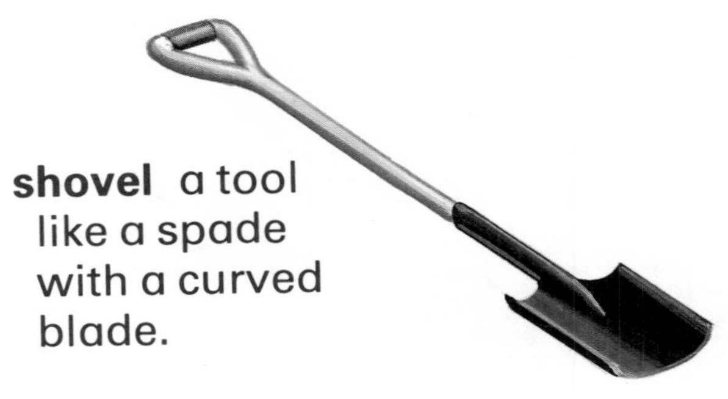

shovel a tool like a spade with a curved blade.

show 1 to point something out.
2 an entertainment, like singing or dancing.

shower
1 a spray of water you stand under to wash yourself.
2 when it rains for a short time.

showjumping a sport where you ride a horse and make it jump over fences. (See *sports*—page 128)

Ss

shrew a small creature like a mouse.

shrimp a small shellfish that you can eat.

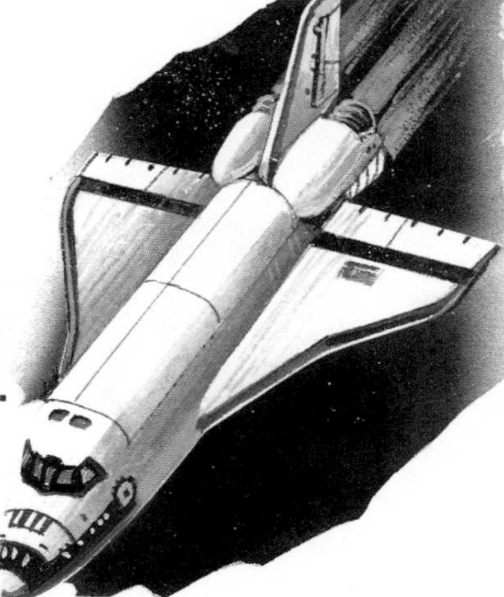

shuttle something that moves quickly to a place and back again, like a space **shuttle.**

sick feeling ill.

side 1 the part of an object that is not the top or the bottom.
2 the edge of something. A square has four **sides.**
3 one of the teams playing in a game.

sideboard a piece of dining room furniture with drawers and small cupboards. You keep things for meals like knives, forks and plates in a **sideboard.**

sieve a wire or plastic net you use to separate solid things from liquids or thick things from fine things.

signal a message given by signs. A red traffic **signal** means stop.

signpost a notice on a post giving people information or directions.

silence no sound. The teacher called for **silence** in class.

silk a shiny material made from the fine thread spun by **silk**worms.

silver a shiny metal that is valuable.

simple 1 easy to do.
2 plain and undecorated.

singer someone who uses their voice to make a tune.

sink 1 a place with taps where you wash the dishes.
2 to go under the water and stay there.

sip to drink a little at a time.

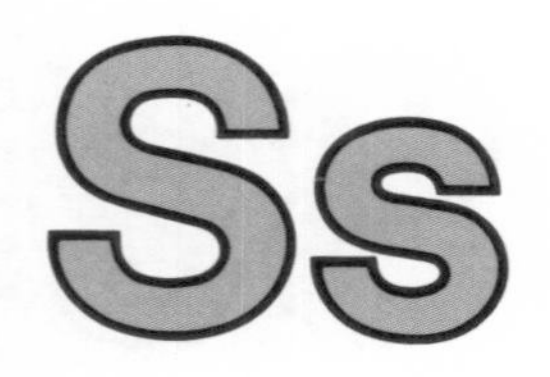

siren an instrument like a horn that makes a loud wailing noise to warn people. The **siren** on an ambulance warns people to get out of the way.

sister a girl or woman who has the same mother and father as the other children in a family.

size how big or how small a thing is. What **size** shoes do you wear?

skate to move along on ice **skates** or roller **skates.**

skeleton all the bones in your body.

skipping rope a rope with a handle at each end. You swing the rope over your head and jump over it as it comes down.

skirt a piece of clothing which hangs down from the waist.

skis two long pieces of wood or metal that you wear to travel over snow. You fix **skis** to your boots to glide along.
(See *transport* – page 141)

skittle one of a set of wooden pieces shaped like bottles. You must roll a ball to knock down as many **skittles** as you can.

skull the bony part of the head.

skunk a small black and white furry animal that gives off a nasty smell when it is in danger.

sky the space up above where you can see clouds, sun, moon and stars.

skyscraper a very tall building.

sledge a frame on wooden or metal runners that you can pull along the snow.

sledgehammer a very heavy hammer for breaking rock.

Ss

sleep to rest with your eyes closed and not be awake.

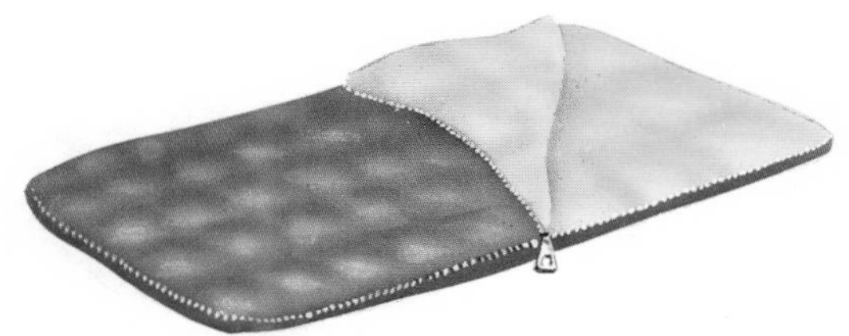

sleeping bag a warm bag you sleep in when you are camping.

sleeve the part of your clothes that covers your arm.

slice a thin piece cut from something larger. Sally cut the loaf into twenty **slices.**

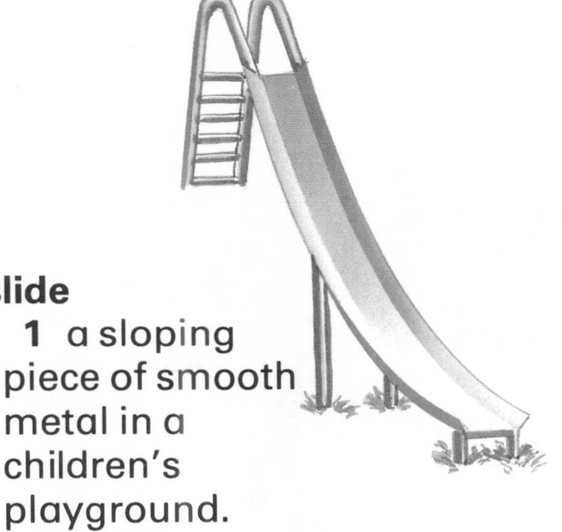

slide
1 a sloping piece of smooth metal in a children's playground.
2 a clip you can wear in your hair.
3 to move smoothly.

sling a cloth tied around your neck and shoulder to hold your arm in place when it is injured.

slip to slide and stumble when you do not expect to do so.

slippers soft shoes you wear indoors.

slow not moving quickly.

slug a small creature like a snail without a shell.

smile to show on your face that you are happy.

smoke **1** the dark cloud from something burning.
2 to breathe in and blow out smoke from a cigar or a cigarette.

smooth flat and even.

smuggler someone who takes things into a country without paying tax on them.

snail a small creature that moves along very slowly and carries its shell on its back.

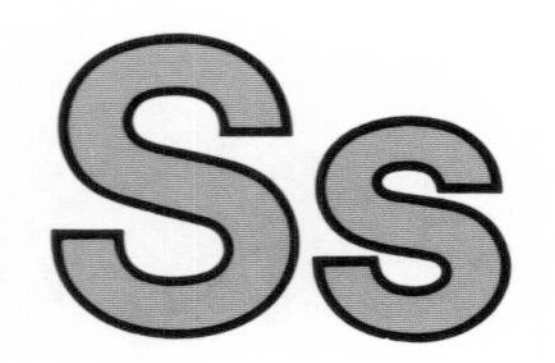

sneeze a sudden noisy rush of air from your nose and mouth. You **sneeze** when you have a tickle inside your nose.

snooker a game played by two people on a special table using coloured balls and sticks called cues.

snore to breathe noisily when you are asleep.

snorkel a tube used by swimmers for breathing while under water. One end of the **snorkel** is above the water and the other end is in the swimmer's mouth.

snowman snow made into the shape of a man.

snowplough a vehicle for clearing snow off the road.

soap a substance used with water for washing and cleaning.

soccer another name for the game of football.

sock a covering for your foot and part of your leg.

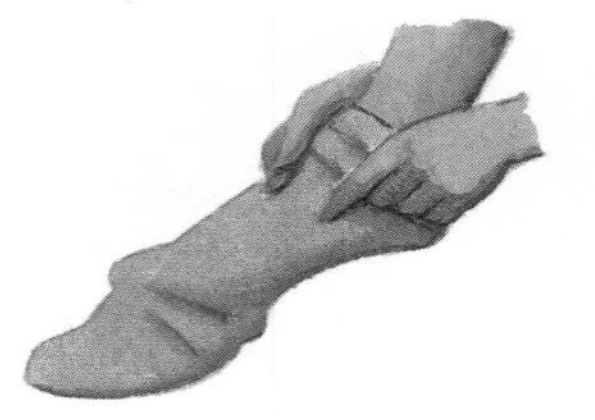

sofa a long comfortable seat for more than one person.

soft **1** not hard. A pillow is **soft** to lie on.
2 not loud. His voice was so **soft** we could hardly hear it.

soil the earth where plants grow.

soldier someone in the army.

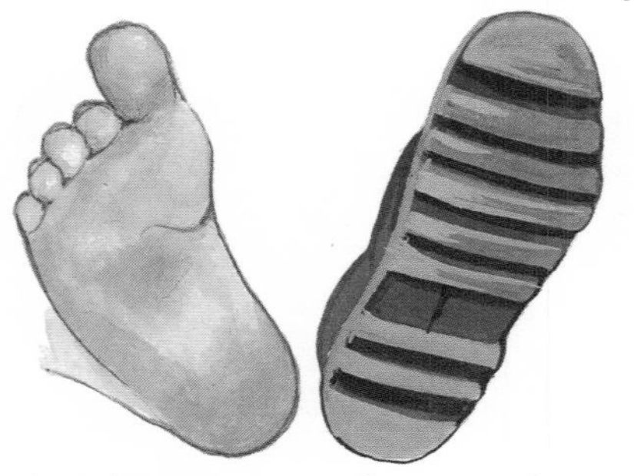

sole the bottom of your foot or shoe.

solid hard and firm.

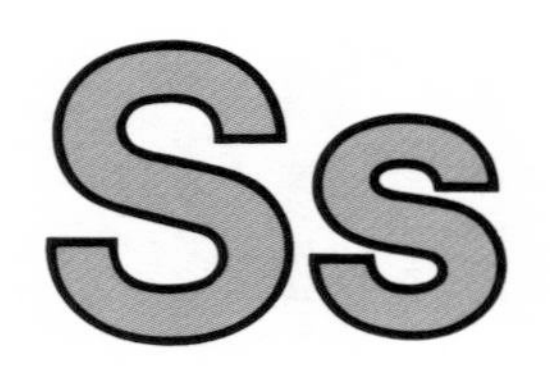

sombrero a big hat that Mexicans wear.

somersault to roll or jump head over heels in the air and land on your feet again.

son a boy child.

sort **1** to put things in the right order or the right group.
2 a kind or type.

S.O.S. the radio signal used by ships and aircraft when calling for help.

sound anything you can hear.

sou'wester a waterproof hat that protects you from the wind and rain.

spacecraft a machine that travels in space.

spade a tool for digging the ground.

spaghetti a food that looks like long pieces of string jumbled together.

spare something which is more than is needed. We carry a **spare** tyre in the back of the car.

spark a piece of something burning that jumps out of a fire.

sparrow a small brown and grey bird that is found all over the world. (See *birds* – page 19)

speak to say something.

spear a pointed stick once used as a weapon.

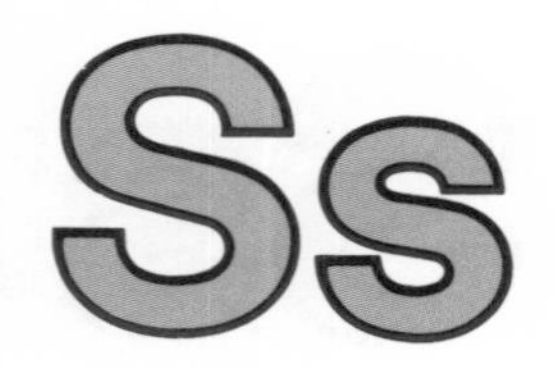

special different from anything else.

spectacles glasses to help you see better.

speedometer an instrument in a vehicle that tells you how fast you are travelling.

spell **1** to say the letters of a word in the right order.
2 magic words that witches and wizards say.

spend to pay out money for things. Johnny often **spends** his pocket money all at once.

spider a small creature with eight legs. **Spiders** spin a web to catch insects.

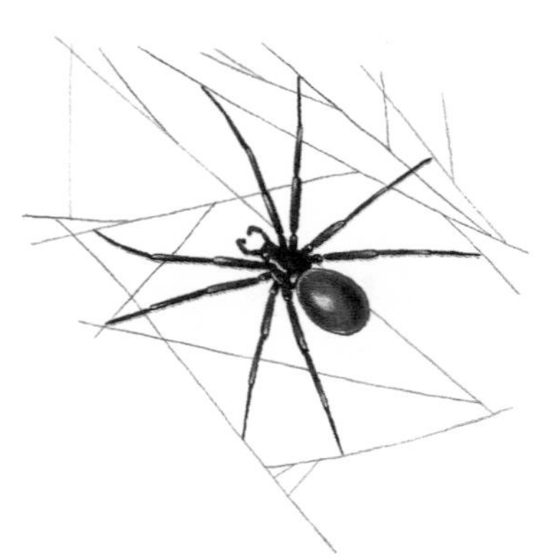

spill to tip something out of a container by accident. I knocked the glass and my milk **spilled** all over the floor.

spin **1** to go round and round very quickly.
2 to make threads of material by twisting it in a machine.

spinach a dark green vegetable you can cook and eat.

spine the backbone of a person or an animal.

spinning wheel a machine worked by a pedal for spinning thread or wool.

spire a tall pointed roof on a church tower.

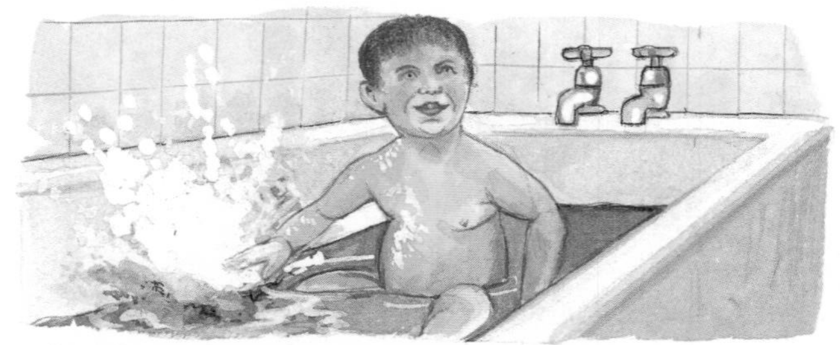

splash to throw liquid about. Jim **splashed** water all over the bathroom walls.

splashdown the dropping of a space capsule into the sea after a space flight.

spoil to damage something so that it is useless.

sponge **1** a soft thick object with holes in. **Sponges** soak up water for washing yourself with.
2 a soft light cake.

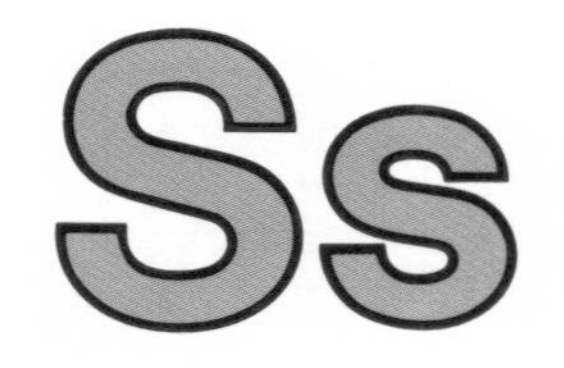

spoon a tool that is like a small bowl on a handle. **Spoons** are used for stirring and eating with.

sport games that give you exercise. Swimming, football and tennis are **sports.** (See page 128)

spread 1 to stretch something out.
2 to cover a surface.

spring 1 the time of year between winter and summer.
2 a jump in the air.
3 a small stream of water that comes up from the ground.
4 a coil of metal.

springboard a plank on the side of a swimming pool. You dive into the water from a **springboard.**

spur a sharp piece of metal worn by horse riders on the heel of their boots. A rider digs the **spur** into the horse's side to make it go faster.

spy 1 someone who secretly watches what other people are doing.
2 to spot something. I **spy** a rabbit by that tree.

square 1 a shape with four straight sides of equal length.
2 a place in a town where four streets make the shape of a **square.**

squash 1 to squeeze something into a different shape.
2 an indoor sport played with a racket and a small round ball.
3 a fruit drink.

squaw the wife of an American Indian.

squeeze to press something hard.

squirrel a small red or grey animal with a bushy tail. **Squirrels** run up and down trees.

stable a building where horses are kept.

stadium a huge place where people watch games and sports.

stage the raised place in a theatre where the show takes place.

stagecoach a large passenger coach pulled by horses. **Stagecoaches** were used in the old days for travelling about the country.

sports

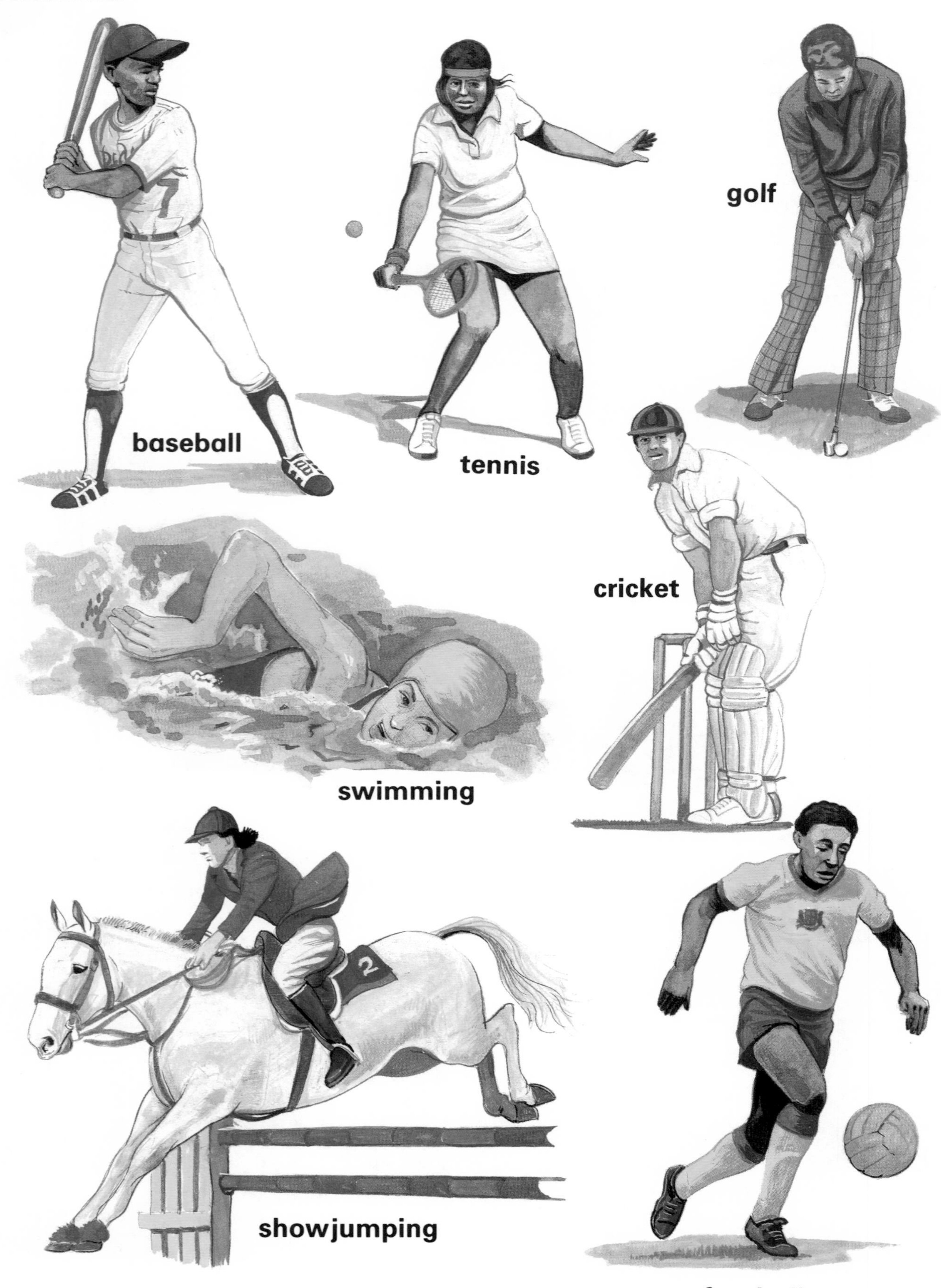
baseball
tennis
golf
cricket
swimming
showjumping
football
7
2

Ss

stairs the steps between floors in a building.

stamp a small piece of paper with a picture on it. You stick **stamps** on letters and parcels to show you have paid to post them.

star
1 one of the bright lights in the night sky.
2 a famous singer or actor.

stare to look hard at someone or something.

starfish a sea creature shaped like a star. You can often find **starfish** on the beach.

station a place where a train stops to let you get on or off.

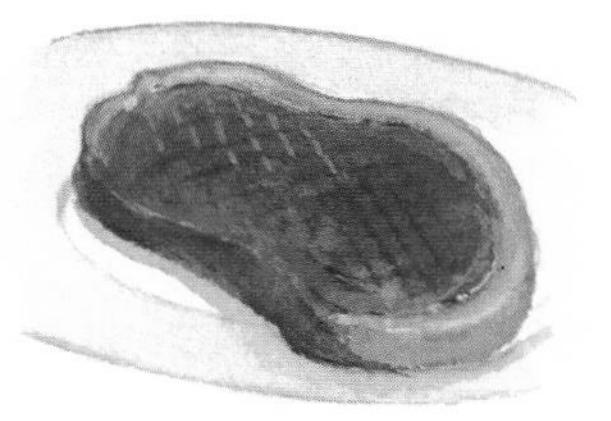

steak a thick slice of meat you fry or grill and then eat.

steal to take something that does not belong to you.

steam the white cloud that rises from boiling water.

steel a very strong metal made from iron.

steep sloping sharply. The hill gets very **steep** at the top.

stem the long thin part of a plant that the flowers and leaves grow from.

step **1** a pace.
2 one of the flat parts of a staircase that you tread on.

stereo a sound that comes from two different places at once.

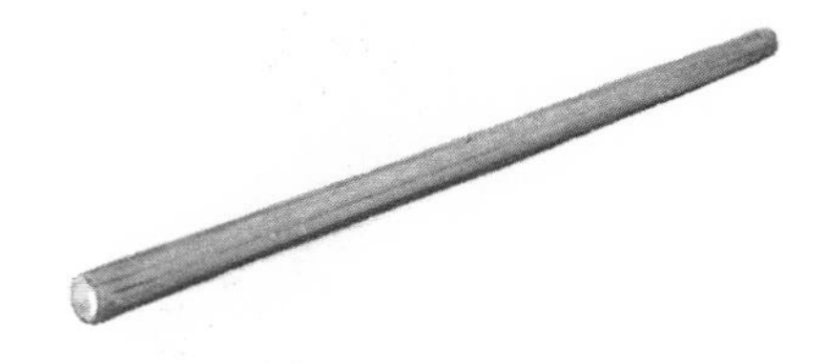

stick **1** a long thin piece of wood.
2 to fix things together with glue.

sting the sharp pricking pain you can get from some insects and plants.

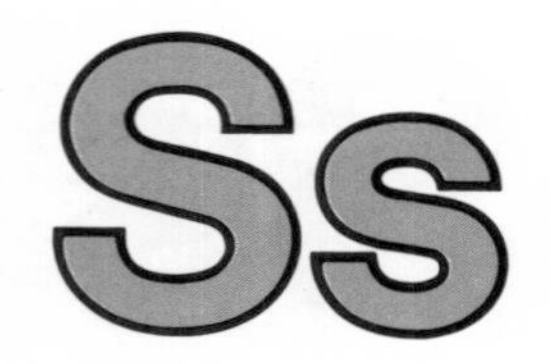

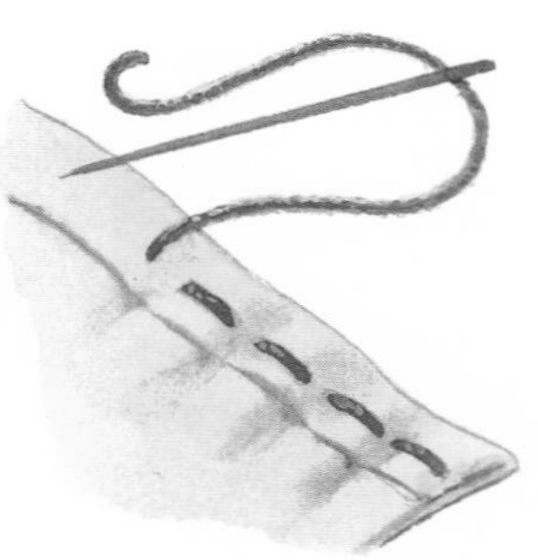

stitch a loop of thread made in sewing.

stomach the part inside your body where the food you eat goes.

stone 1 a small piece of rock.
2 the hard seed inside some fruit like peaches and plums.

stool a small seat with no back.

stopwatch a watch that you can start and stop easily. You can use a **stopwatch** to measure exactly how long someone has taken to run a race.

store 1 a large shop.
2 to keep something for later. We **store** apples in the garage.

stork a big bird with long legs and a long neck.

storm rough weather with heavy wind and rain.

story a tale that may be made up or one that really happened.

straight not curved.

strange unusual.

strap a long thin piece of material. **Straps** are used for fastening things together.

straw 1 a long thin tube made of paper or plastic. You suck a drink through a **straw.**
2 dried stalks of corn.

strawberry a soft red fruit with a sweet taste.

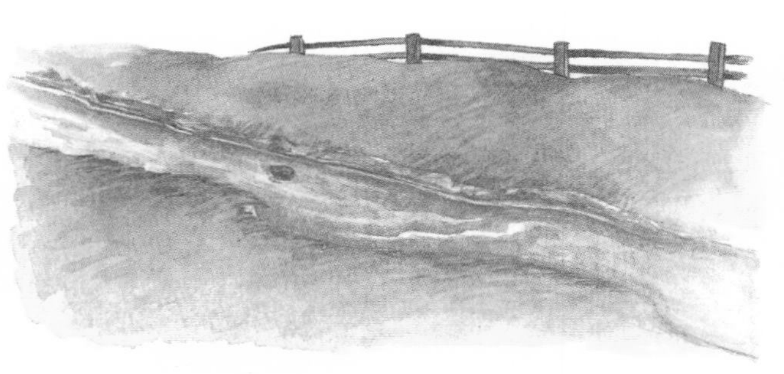

stream a small river.

street a road that has houses and other buildings along both sides.

stretch **1** to make something longer or wider by pulling it.
2 to reach out.

stretcher a kind of bed made of canvas and two poles. **Stretchers** are used to carry injured people.

strike **1** to hit something.
2 to refuse to work.

string very thin rope used for tying things.

strong **1** able to lift heavy things.
2 powerful. We have a **strong** team this year.

study to learn about something.

submarine a special ship that can travel under the sea.

substance what something is made from. Iron is a hard **substance**.

sugar small grains that are used for making food and drinks taste sweet.

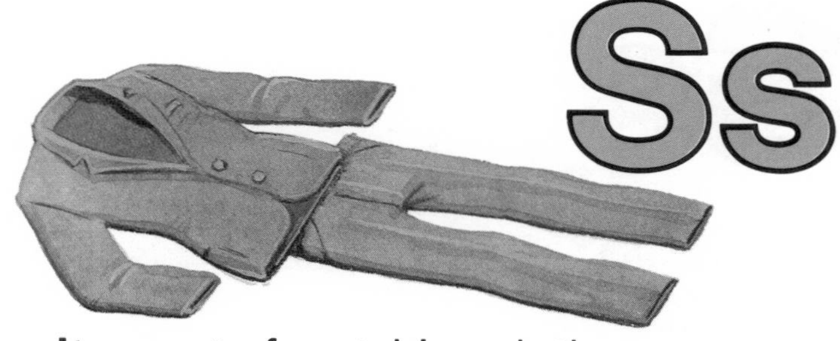

suit a set of matching clothes.

summer the time of year between spring and autumn.

sunflower a large yellow flower on a very tall stem.

sunglasses dark glasses that shade your eyes from the sun.

sunrise when the sun comes up in the morning.

sunset when the sun goes down in the evening.

supermarket a big store where you help yourself to goods and pay for them on the way out.

supersonic moving faster than the speed that sound travels. Some jets travel at **supersonic** speed.

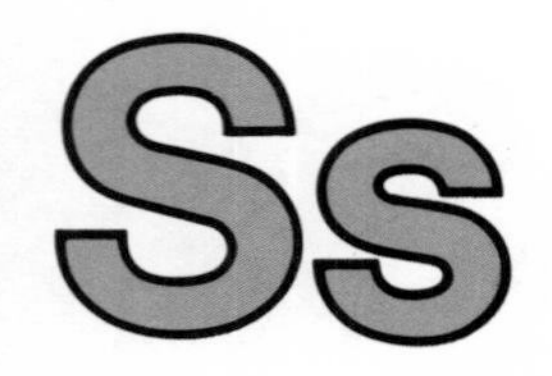

suppose to think something is true.

sure knowing you are right.

surfboard a long board you stand or lie on to glide over waves.

surgeon a doctor who is trained to operate on people.

surprise something pleasant that happens when you did not expect it. The birthday party was a complete **surprise.**

swallow
1 a fast-flying bird with a forked tail.
2 to let food or drink go down your throat into your stomach.

swan a large, usually white bird with a long curving neck. **Swans** are found on rivers and lakes. (See *birds* – page 19)

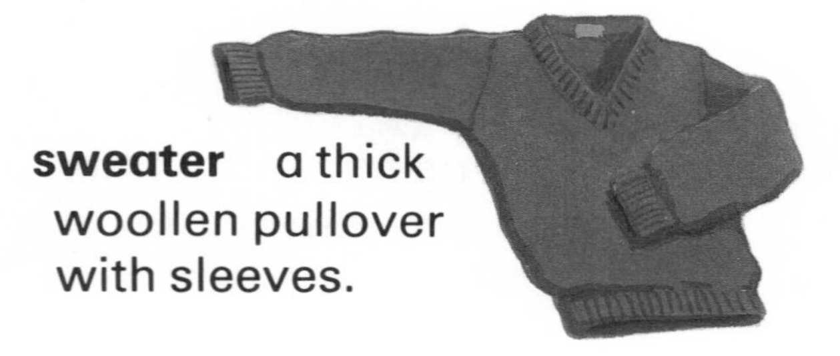

sweater a thick woollen pullover with sleeves.

sweep **1** to clean something with a brush or broom.
2 someone who cleans chimneys.

sweet **1** tasting like sugar.
2 a piece of food made with sugar. Toffees are **sweets.**

swimming moving along in the water using your legs and arms. (See *sports* – page 128)

swing **1** a seat that hangs down on chains or ropes. You sit on the seat and **swing** backwards and forwards.
2 to move backwards and forwards or side to side.

sword (sounds like sord) a weapon like a long knife. A **sword** has a sharp blade on a handle.

swordfish (sounds like sordfish) a large fish with a long sharp jaw that looks like the blade of a sword.

synagogue the church of the Jewish religion.

syrup a sweet sticky liquid.

table a piece of furniture that has a flat top on four legs.

tablecloth a large piece of cloth you use to cover a table for meals.

table tennis a ball game played on a large table with a net. You play **table tennis** with small flat bats and a light ball.

tadpole a baby frog or toad.

tail the part that is at the end of something. Most animals have **tails.**

tailor someone who makes clothes.

talk to speak. My brother **talks** a lot in class.

tall very high. My mother works in a **tall** office block.

tambourine a musical instrument that is like a flat drum with small cymbals around the edge. You can bang or shake a **tambourine** to make music.

tank **1** a strong heavy car used in war. **Tanks** move on tracks and have guns.
2 a large container for water and other liquids.

tap **1** to hit gently.
2 a handle at the end of a pipe that turns water on or off.

tape **1** a thin strip of material. Sticky **tape** is used for fastening parcels.
2 a magnetic ribbon used in cassette players and tape recorders.

tape recorder a machine which can record sounds on tape and then play them back again.

target something you aim at to hit with a bullet from a gun or an arrow from a bow.

tart a piece of pastry with jam or fruit in it.

task a piece of work you have to do.

Tt

taste the flavour of food or drink in your mouth.

tattoo drawings or patterns in colour on your skin.

taxi a car that takes you from one place to another for payment.

tea **1** a hot drink made with boiling water and **tea** leaves.
2 a light meal in the afternoon or evening.

teacher someone who helps you learn at school.

team a group of people who play together on the same side in a game.

tear **1** (rhymes with dear) a drop of water that falls from your eye when you cry.
2 (rhymes with dare) to pull something to pieces.

teddy bear a toy bear.

teeth the hard white bones in your mouth. You use your **teeth** for chewing food.

telephone an instrument that carries voices through wires. You can talk with someone far away on the **telephone.**

telescope a long tube with special glass in it that makes distant objects look closer.

television a box that brings pictures and sounds to you from far away.

temperature the measurement of how hot or cold something is.

tennis a game for two or four people using rackets and soft balls. **Tennis** is played on a court with a net across. (See *sports* – page 128)

tent a shelter made of cloth held up with poles and ropes. People sleep in **tents** when they go camping.

tentacle the long bending arm of some creatures. An octopus has eight **tentacles.**

Tt

test 1 a set of questions to see how much you know about something, like a spelling **test.**
2 to try something out. The mechanic **tested** the engine.

test tube a thin glass tube, closed at one end, that is used by scientists.

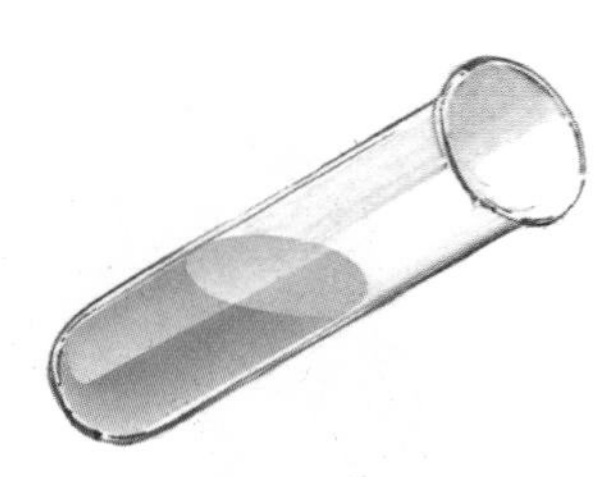

theatre a building where you can see plays and shows.

their belonging to them. She gave the girls **their** books.

there in that place. Stay **there.**

thermometer an instrument that measures temperature.

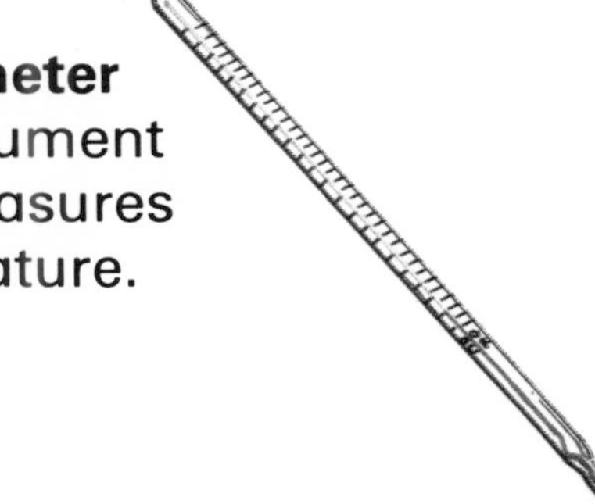

thief someone who takes what belongs to someone else.

thimble a small metal cover for your finger to keep the needle from hurting you when you are sewing.

thin not fat, not thick.

think to use your mind.

thirsty wanting to drink.

thistle a wild plant with prickly leaves.

thorn the sharp points on some flower stems.

thought something that you think.

thread a long thin piece of material you use for sewing with a needle.

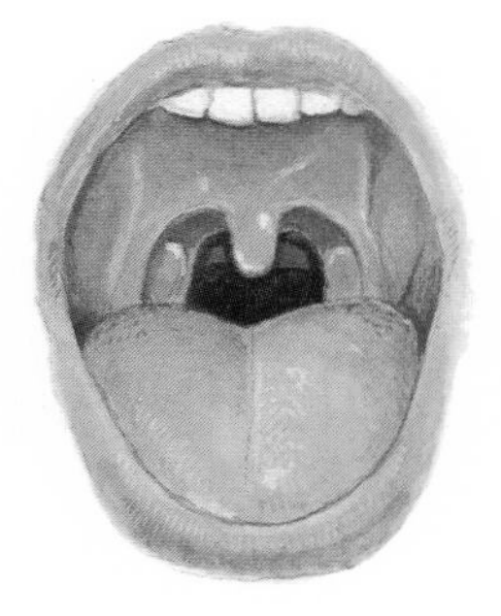

throat the part of your body at the back of your mouth.

Tt

throne a large decorated chair for a king or queen.

through from one end to the other. We have to go **through** the forest to get to the river.

throw to send something into the air using your hand and arm.

thrush a brown spotted bird that has a sweet singing voice. (See *birds* – page 19)

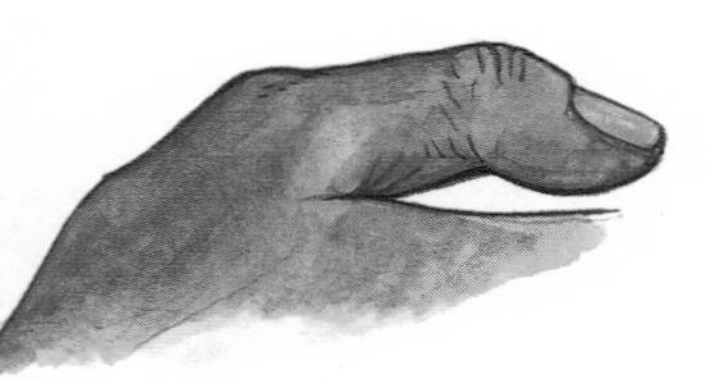

thumb part of your hand that is like a short thick finger.

thunder a loud rumbling noise in the sky during a thunderstorm.

ticket a piece of paper or card that shows you have paid to travel somewhere or to get into somewhere.

tickle to touch someone in a way that makes them laugh.

tide the movement of the sea towards the land and then away again.

tidy neat. Mike keeps his desk very **tidy**.

tie **1** a piece of material you wear around your neck under your collar.
2 to fasten something with a knot.

tiger a fierce striped animal of the cat family.

tightrope a high wire that acrobats perform on at the circus.

tile a kind of flat thin brick for covering roofs, floors and walls.

time **1** a moment in the day.
2 seconds, minutes, hours, days, weeks, months and years.

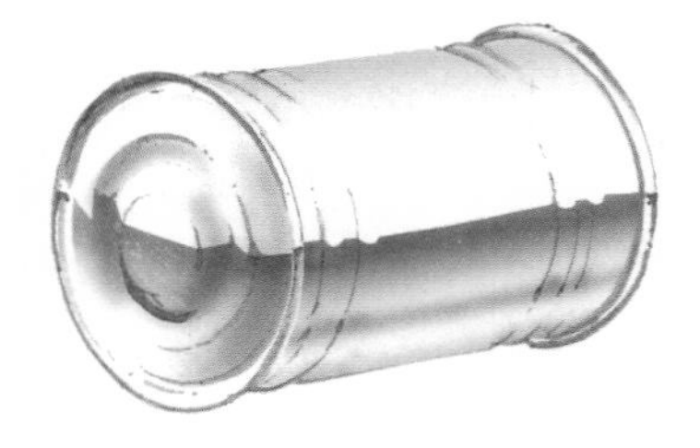

tin **1** a metal can.
2 a silvery metal.

Tt

tingle to have a tickly feeling in your fingers or toes.

tinsel glittering material used for decoration.

tip **1** the pointed end of something.
2 to turn something over so that the things inside fall out.

tiptoe to walk carefully and quietly on your toes.

tissue soft paper for wiping or wrapping things.

toad an animal like a frog but with rougher skin. **Toads** live on land most of the time.

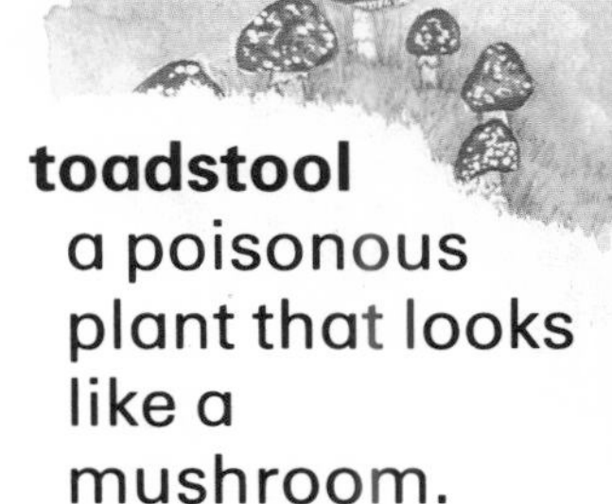

toadstool a poisonous plant that looks like a mushroom.

toast bread that has been cooked until it is brown and crisp.

tobacco dried leaves of the **tobacco** plant that are cut up. People smoke **tobacco** in cigarettes, pipes and cigars.

toboggan a long flat-bottomed sledge for sliding down snowy slopes.

today this day.

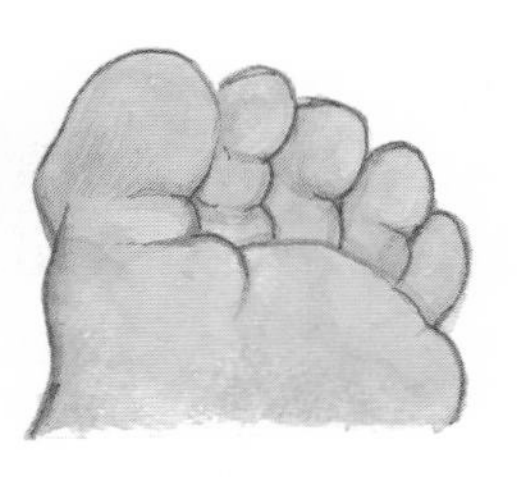

toe one of the five parts at the end of each foot.

toffee a sticky chewy sweet made from sugar and butter.

together with other people or other things. Put all your toys **together** in the box.

tomahawk a kind of axe used by American Indians.

tomato a soft red fruit with pips in. **Tomatoes** are eaten raw or cooked.

Tt

tom tom
a drum you play by beating it with your hands.

tongs a tool with two claws used for lifting things like lumps of sugar or coal.

tongue (sounds like tung) the piece of flesh inside your mouth which moves when you talk or eat.

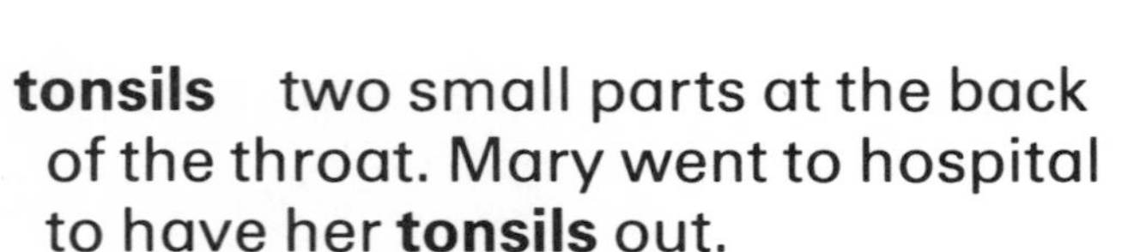

tonsils two small parts at the back of the throat. Mary went to hospital to have her **tonsils** out.

tool an instrument that helps you to do work.

tool box
a place where tools are kept.

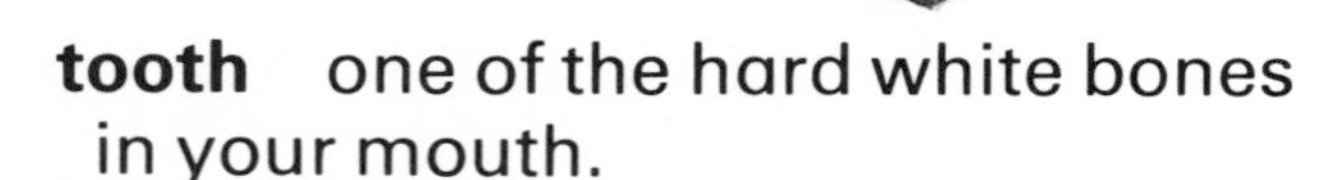

tooth one of the hard white bones in your mouth.

toothbrush
a small brush with a handle you clean your teeth with.

toothpaste a paste you squeeze from a tube on to a toothbrush for cleaning your teeth.

top **1** a toy which spins round fast.
2 the highest part of something or somewhere. We can see the **top** of the mountain.

torch a light you can carry in your hand.

torpedo a kind of bomb that travels under water and explodes when it hits its target.

tortoise an animal with a thick shell on its back, which walks very slowly. (See *animals* – page 11)

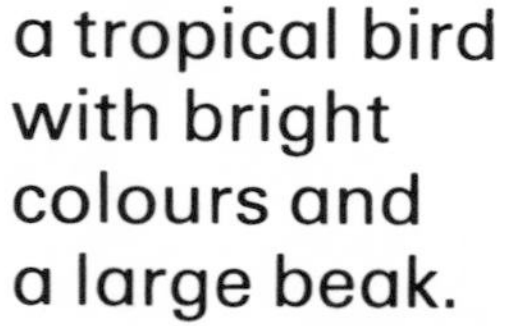

toucan
a tropical bird with bright colours and a large beak.

touch to feel something with your fingers.

tour a journey where you visit many different places.

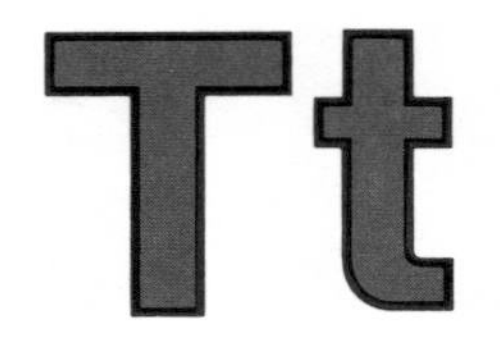

towards in the direction of. The bird was flying **towards** the window.

towel a cloth you use to dry things with.

tower a tall building.

trace to copy a picture by drawing its outline on transparent paper.

track 1 the marks left by a person or an animal.
2 a railway line.
3 a narrow rough path.

tractor a machine on the farm that pulls a plough or a trailer. (See *machines* – page 78)

trade 1 to buy and sell things.
2 the kind of work people do.

traffic vehicles like cars, buses and trucks moving along the road.

traffic lights lights that control the traffic at crossings.

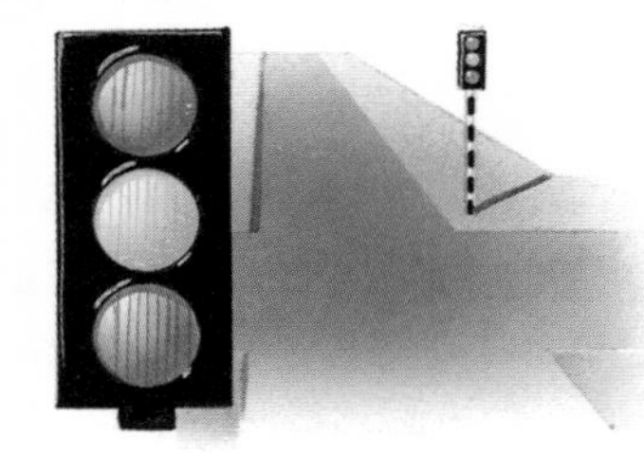

trail tracks made by the footprints of people or animals.

trailer an open cart on wheels pulled by another vehicle. **Trailers** are used for carrying loads.

train 1 railway carriages pulled by an engine. (See *transport* – page 141)
2 to practise to do a sport.

tram a kind of bus which runs on railway lines in the road and is attached to cables overhead.

tramp someone without a home who wanders from place to place.

trampoline a sheet of strong material fastened to a frame with springs. You can bounce up and down on a **trampoline**.

transfer 1 to move something from one place to another.
2 a picture that can be moved from paper on to something else.

Tt

transparent easy to see through. Jars are **transparent** so that you can see what is in them.

transport different kinds of vehicles that carry people and goods from one place to another. (See page 141)

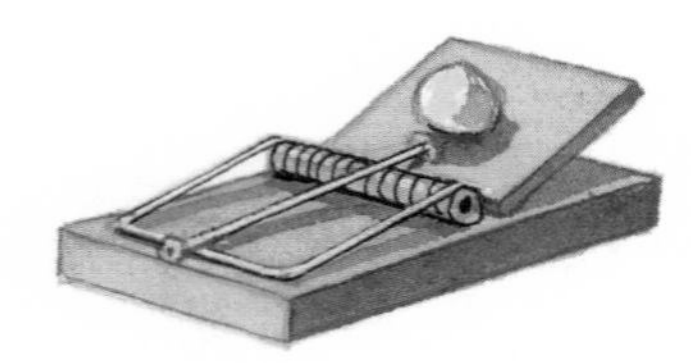

trap **1** something to catch animals in, like a mouse **trap** or an elephant **trap**.
2 to capture a person or an animal by using a trick.

trapeze a swing high in the air at the circus. Acrobats perform daring tricks on the **trapeze**.

travel agent someone who arranges holidays for people.

tray a flat piece of wood, metal or plastic for carrying food and drinks.

treacle a thick, sweet, sticky liquid used in cooking.

treasure something of great value like gold, silver and jewels.

tree a large plant with a trunk, branches and leaves.

trench a long narrow ditch dug in the ground.

triangle a shape with three straight sides.

trick something clever that is done to fool you. Magicians can do amazing **tricks**.

tricycle a cycle with three wheels.

trigger the part of a gun you have to pull to make it fire.

trip **1** a short journey. We went on a **trip** to the museum.
2 to catch your foot on something and fall over.

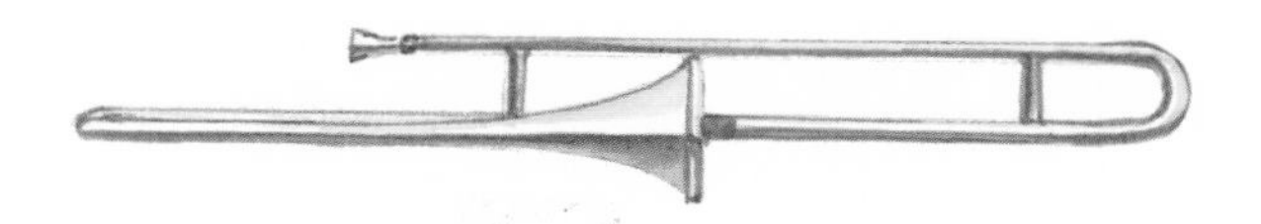

trombone a musical instrument made of a brass tube. You play the **trombone** by blowing into it and sliding part of the tube.

transport

balloon

skis

aeroplane

car

ship

train

Tt

trot to run slowly. The horse **trotted** along the path.

trouble something that makes you worried or unhappy.

trousers a piece of clothing that covers your legs.

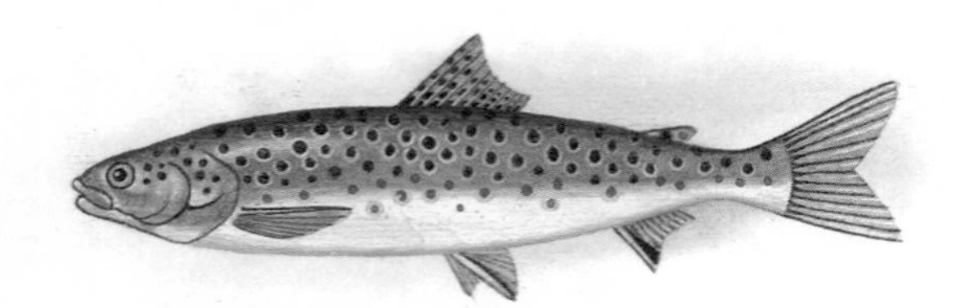

trout a fish that lives in rivers and lakes.

truck a large vehicle that carries heavy loads.

true correct or real.

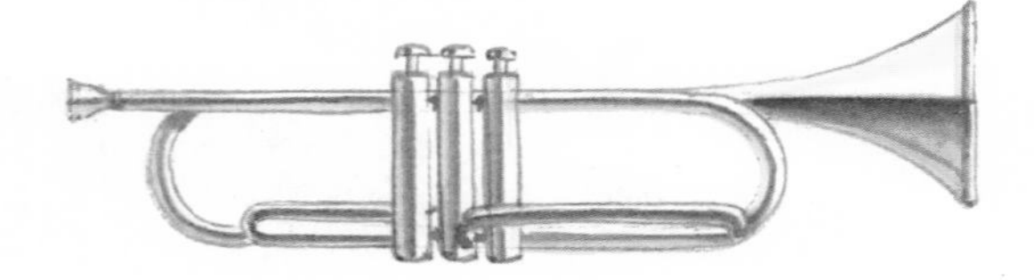

trumpet a brass musical instrument you play by blowing.

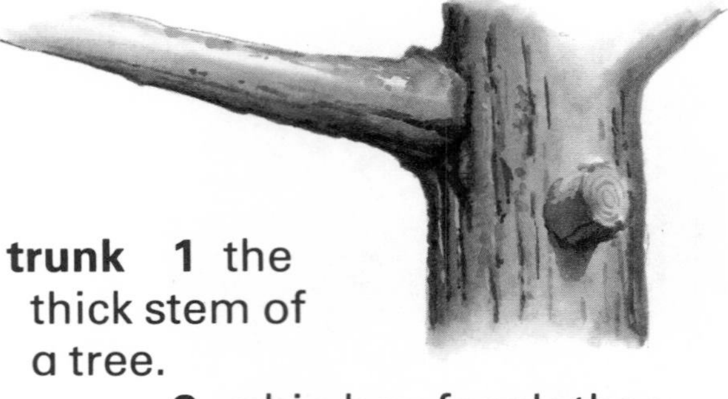

trunk **1** the thick stem of a tree.
2 a big box for clothes.
3 the long, curling nose of an elephant.

try **1** to make an effort to do something.
2 to test something. Sally will **try** the dress to see if it fits.

T-shirt a light shirt with short sleeves that is shaped like a T.

tuba a large brass musical instrument that makes deep notes when you blow into it.

tug to give something a sharp pull.

tugboat a small but powerful boat that pulls other boats.

tulip a brightly coloured flower that is grown from a bulb.

tumble to fall over.

Tt

tune musical notes made into a piece of music.

tunnel a long hole through a mountain or under the ground.

turban a covering for the head made by wrapping a piece of cloth in a special way.

turkey a large bird that is often eaten at Christmas.

turn 1 to swing around to face a different way.
2 to change. Tadpoles **turn** into frogs.
3 someone's go. It is Steve's **turn** to throw the dice.

turnip a vegetable that grows underground. You can cook and eat **turnips.**

turtle an animal like a tortoise with a shell on its back. **Turtles** live in water most of the time.

tusk a long pointed tooth found in some animals. Elephants have **tusks.**

twice two times. The postman knocked **twice** at the door.

twig a small branch of a tree.

twins two babies born at the same time from the same mother.

twist to turn something round and round.

type 1 one kind. What **type** of cheese do you like?
2 to print letters and numbers on paper using a machine.

typewriter a machine with keys that you press to type with.

typist someone whose job is to use a typewriter.

Uu

udder the part of a cow where milk comes from.

ugly not pretty.

ukulele a musical instrument like a small guitar.

umbrella a metal frame covered with cloth. You hold an **umbrella** over your head to keep off the rain.

umpire someone who judges between two sides in games like tennis and cricket.

uncle the brother of your mother or father, or the husband of your aunt.

uncomfortable not comfortable. The broken springs make the chair very **uncomfortable.**

under below.

undercarriage the wheels of an aircraft used for taking off and landing.

underground 1 under the ground.
2 a railway that runs through tunnels under a city.

underpass a path or road built to go under another road.

understand to know what something means.

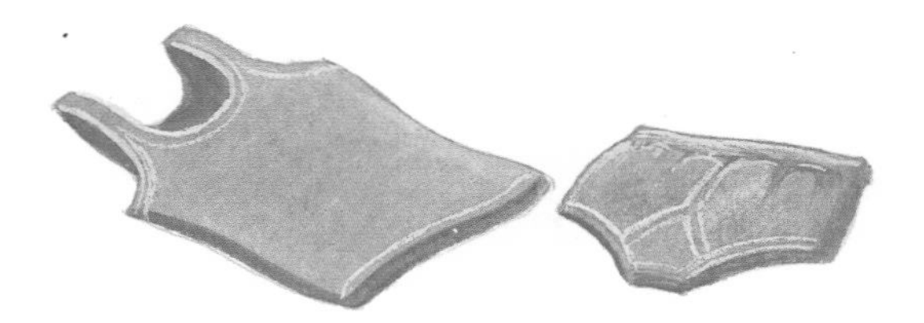

underwear clothes you wear under your top clothes.

undress to take off your clothes.

unhappy sad.

unicorn a fairy-tale animal like a horse with one straight horn coming out of its head.

Uu

uniform special clothes worn by people in the same group. Soldiers, sailors, nurses and the police wear **uniforms.**

union a group of workers who join together as a group.

unit an amount used in measuring or counting. Metres are **units** of length.

unite to join together for a purpose.

universe everything on earth and in space.

university a place where people can go on studying when they leave school.

unless if not. You will not catch the train **unless** you run.

until up to a particular time. I must wear the bandage **until** the cut has healed.

upholstery padding and covering for chairs and settees.

upside down the wrong way up.

upstairs the rooms in a building that you reach by climbing the stairs.

urgent something that must be done at once.

useful helpful.

usher someone who shows you to your seat in church or in a theatre.

usual happening very often. Jane was late for school as **usual.**

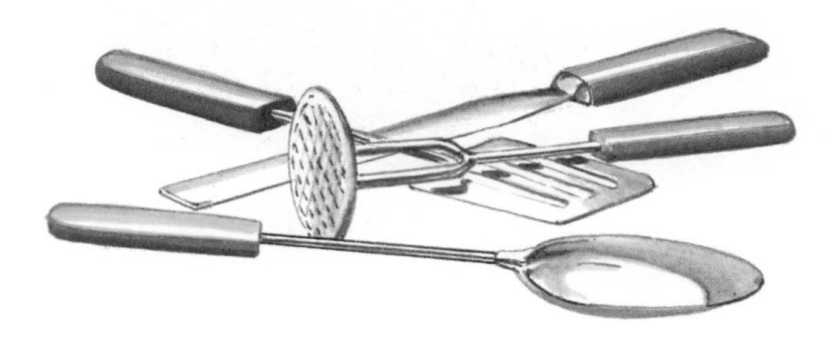

utensil any household tool.

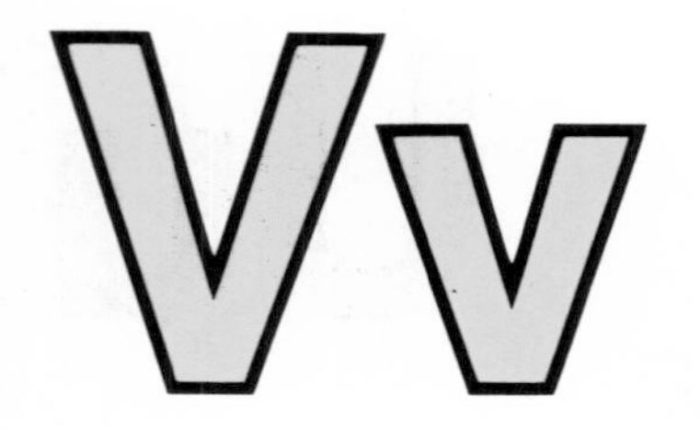

vacant empty. The train was so crowded there was not one **vacant** seat.

vacation time off from school or work, or a trip for pleasure.

vaccination an injection to stop you catching certain illnesses.

vacuum cleaner a machine for sucking up dust and dirt from carpets and floors.

valentine a card with a loving message you send to someone on St Valentine's Day, February 14th.

valley low land that lies between hills or mountains.

van a kind of car for carrying goods.

vanish to disappear.

various of different kinds. There are **various** things I want to do this week.

vase a pot or jar you put flowers in.

vault **1** a kind of jump in sports, like a pole **vault**.
2 an underground room.

vegetable a plant that is grown for food.

vehicle anything that carries people or goods over land. Bicycles, cars and buses are **vehicles.**

vein a narrow tube that carries blood round your body to your heart.

velvet a heavy kind of cloth that is soft and smooth to touch.

verse part of a poem or song.

Vv

vessel **1** a container for liquid.
2 a boat or ship.

vest a piece of underwear that covers the top part of your body.

vet someone whose job is to help sick animals get well again.

viaduct a long bridge that carries a road or railway across a valley.

vicar a religious man in charge of a church.

video pictures and sounds recorded on tape that you play back on a television screen.

view **1** what you can see around you.
2 an opinion.

village a small town.

vine the plant that grapes grow on.

violin a musical instrument with four strings that you play using a bow.

visit to go to see a person or a place.

visor the part of a helmet that protects your face.

voice the sounds people make when they speak or sing.

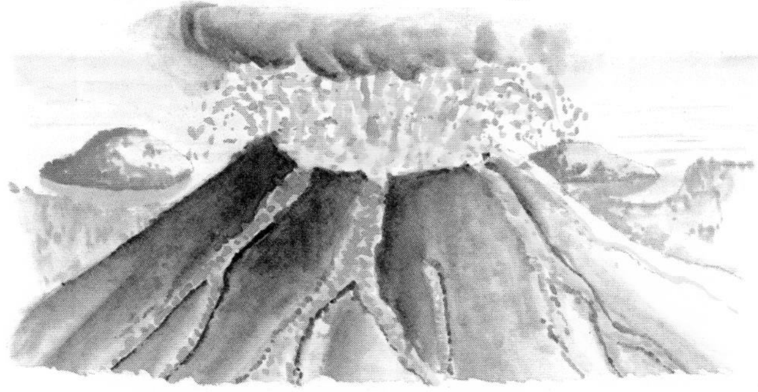

volcano a mountain that sometimes explodes at the top. **Volcanoes** can throw out hot ash and lava when they explode.

voyage a long journey made by boat.

vulture a large fierce bird that eats dead animals.

Ww

wagon
 1 a cart that carries heavy loads.
 2 a railway truck carrying goods.

waist the middle part of your body below your ribs.

waiter someone who brings your food in a restaurant.

wake to stop sleeping.

walk to travel on foot.

wallet a small pocket case of leather or plastic for carrying money and papers.

wallpaper rolls of paper with patterns on them. You cover the walls of a room with **wallpaper**.

walnut a nut with a very hard shell.

walrus a sea creature like a big seal with two tusks.

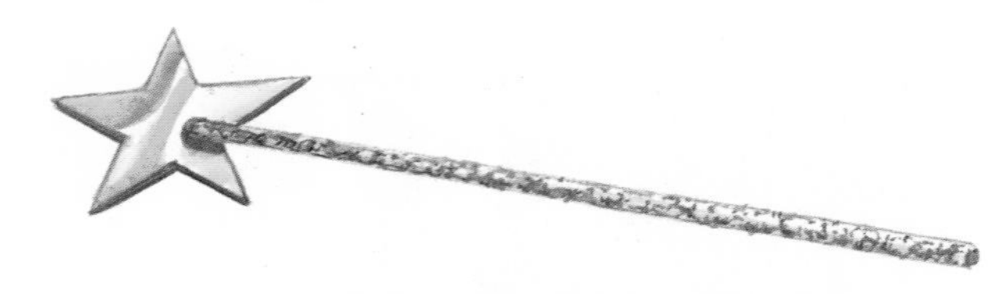

wand a thin stick used by witches and wizards to cast spells.

wander to walk along with no special place to go.

want to wish to have something.

wardrobe a tall cupboard you keep clothes in.

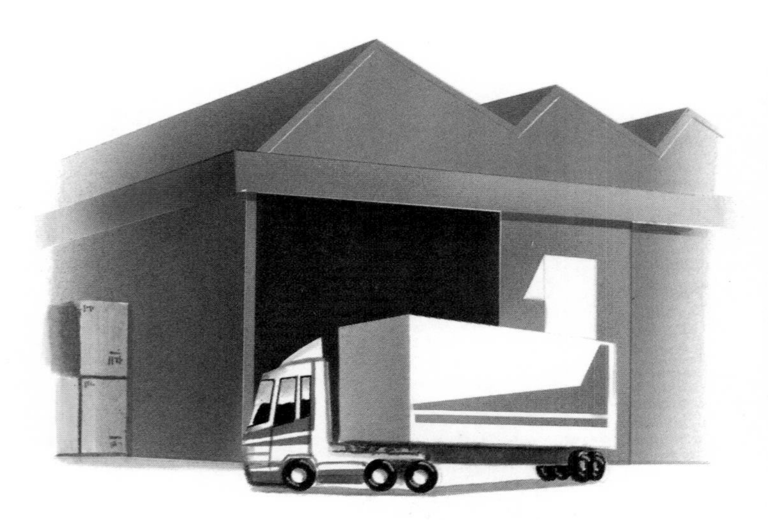

warehouse a large building where goods are stored.

warm more hot than cold.

warn to tell someone they are in danger.

warrior someone in olden times who fought battles.

washing machine a machine for washing clothes.

wasp an insect that has black and yellow stripes and can sting you.

waste to use more of something than you need.

watch 1 a small clock on a strap you wear on your wrist.
2 to look carefully at someone or something.

water the liquid in streams, rivers, lakes and seas.

waterfall a stream of water that pours down from a high place.

waterproof made of a material that does not let water through. I wear my **waterproof** coat when it rains.

water-skier someone who glides over water on a pair of skis. The **water-skier** is pulled along by a fast boat.

wave 1 a moving line of water on the surface of the sea.
2 to move your hand to say goodbye.

wax a soft thick substance used to make candles and polish.

weak not strong.

wear to be dressed in something.

weasel a small thin animal which runs fast and eats rats, mice and birds' eggs.

Ww

weather the state of the air outside. Rain, sun, wind, snow are all different kinds of **weather.**

weathervane a piece of metal which swings around in the wind to show which way it is blowing.

weave to make threads into cloth.

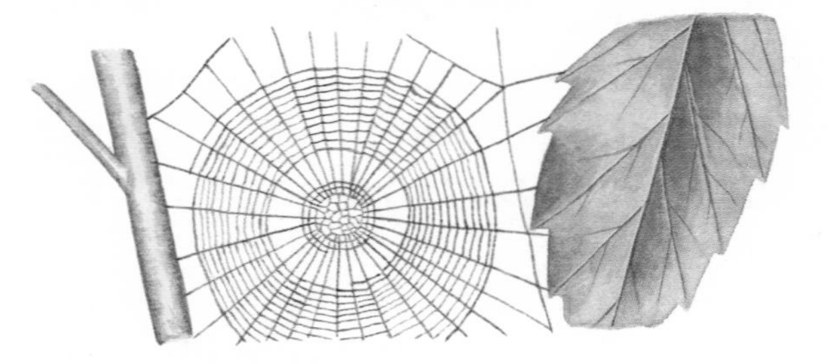

web the very fine net a spider makes to catch insects for food.

web-footed the kind of foot a duck has where the toes are joined by skin.

wedding the time when a man and a woman get married.

week seven days.

weekend the time from Friday evening to Sunday evening.

weigh to find out how heavy something is.

welcome to show someone that you are pleased they have come to see you.

well **1** a deep hole dug in the ground to reach water or oil.
2 healthy.

wet not dry.

whale a very big sea animal.

wheat a kind of grain. **Wheat** is used for making flour.

wheel a large circle of wood or metal fixed in the middle so that it can turn.

wheelbarrow a small cart you can push. **Wheelbarrows** have two handles and a wheel at the front.

wheelchair a chair on large wheels. People who cannot walk far travel in **wheelchairs.**

whip a length of cord or leather fixed to a handle.

whiskers **1** the long stiff hairs that grow near the mouth of some animals. Cats and mice have **whiskers.**
2 the stiff hairs that grow on a man's face.

whisper to speak very quietly.

whistle
1 a small instrument you blow into to make a sharp sound.
2 to make a clear sharp sound by blowing air through your lips when they are almost closed.

wicket the three stumps with two bails on top in the game of cricket.

width how wide something is.

wife a woman who is married.

wig a piece of false hair to cover your head.

wild **1** not tame.
2 fierce.

willow a tree with drooping branches. **Willows** often grow near water.

wind **1** (rhymes with tinned) air that moves quickly.
2 (rhymes with find) to turn round and round.

windmill a machine with sails that are turned by the wind. **Windmills** are used to grind corn or pump water.

window a hole in the wall of a building that is covered with glass. **Windows** let in light and air.

windscreen the front window of a vehicle.

Ww

wine a strong drink made from grapes.

wing the part of the body of birds and insects which they use to fly.

winter the time of year between autumn and spring.

wire a long thin piece of metal. Some kinds of **wire** carry electricity.

wise understanding many things.

wishbone the bone from a chicken or turkey that is shaped like a V. The two ends of a **wishbone** are pulled apart for luck.

witch a woman in a fairy tale who can do magic.

wizard a man in a fairy tale who can do magic.

wobble to move shakily from side to side like a jelly.

wolf a wild animal that looks like a big dog.

woman a girl who has grown up.

wonderful so good that it surprises you.

wood **1** a small forest of trees. **2** the substance found under the bark of trees.

woodpecker a bird that uses its beak to make holes in a tree.

woodwork making things out of wood.

woodworm a small beetle that nibbles through wood.

Ww

wool the thick hair of a sheep that can be spun into woollen thread. Some kinds of cloth are made from **wool.**

word letters put together to make something you can say or read.

work doing or making something.

workshop a building where things are made.

world our planet and all the people and things on it.

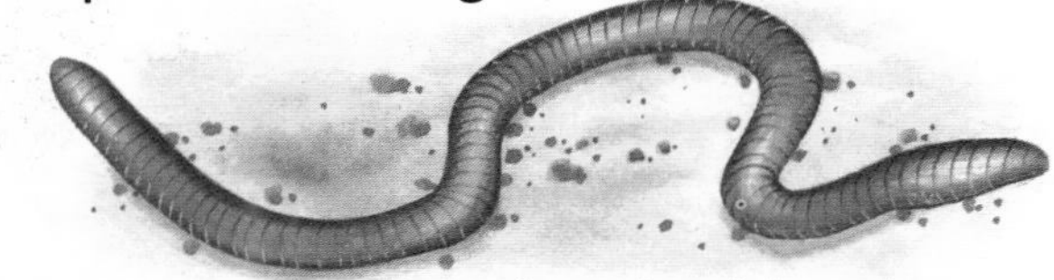

worm a small animal with a long thin body. **Worms** live underground.

wound (sounds like woond) an injury.

wrap to cover something all over with cloth or paper.

wreck **1** something damaged that cannot be mended.
2 to damage something badly.

wren a very small brown bird that sings sweetly. (See *birds* – page 19)

wrestler someone who takes part in the sport where two people struggle to force each other to the ground.

wrinkle a crease in a piece of cloth or in your skin.

wrist the joint between your hand and your arm.

write to put words or figures on paper so that people can read them.

wrong **1** not a good thing to do. It is **wrong** to take something that does not belong to you.
2 not correct. It is **wrong** to say that 2 + 2 equals 5.

x-ray a special kind of photograph that shows what the inside of your body looks like.

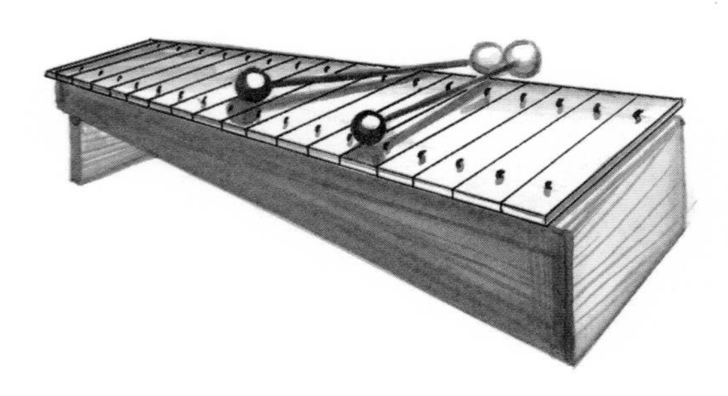

xylophone a musical instrument made of bars of wood or metal. The player hits the bars with small wooden hammers.

yacht a boat with large sails.

yak an animal like an ox with long hair.

yard 1 a small piece of ground with walls around it.
2 a measurement of length. There are three feet in a **yard.**

yarn 1 woollen thread used for knitting and weaving.
2 a long story.

yashmak a piece of cloth worn over the face by some Muslim women.

yawn to open your mouth wide and breathe in when you are sleepy.

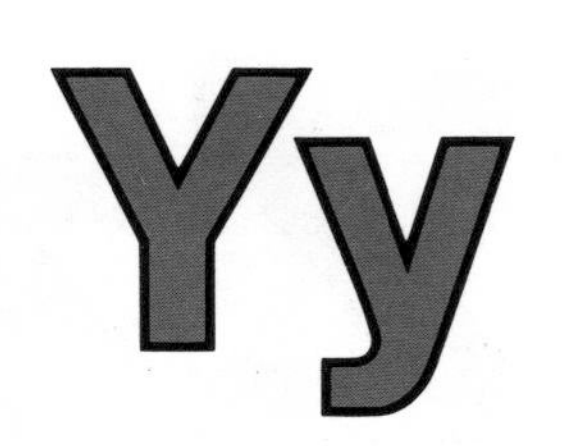

yeast a plant used in making bread that helps it rise when it is baking.

yell to cry out very loudly.

yellowhammer a bird with a yellow head and chest.

yesterday the day before today.

yeti a large hairy animal that some people believe lives in the mountains.

yew a kind of tree that stays green all the year.

yodel to sing very loudly changing from high notes to low notes and back again.

yoga a set of exercises that are good for your body and your mind.

yoghurt a thick liquid made from sour milk. Sometimes **yoghurt** is flavoured with fruit.

yoke a curved piece of wood that is fixed to a cart. The **yoke** fits over the necks of two oxen to help them pull the cart.

yolk the yellow part of an egg.

young not old; not yet grown up. A kitten is a **young** cat.

youth hostel a place where young people on holiday can stay the night for very little money.

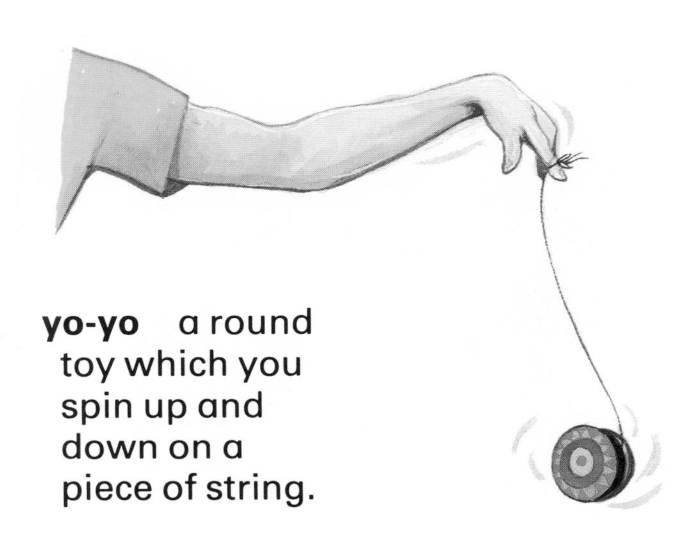

yo-yo a round toy which you spin up and down on a piece of string.

Zz

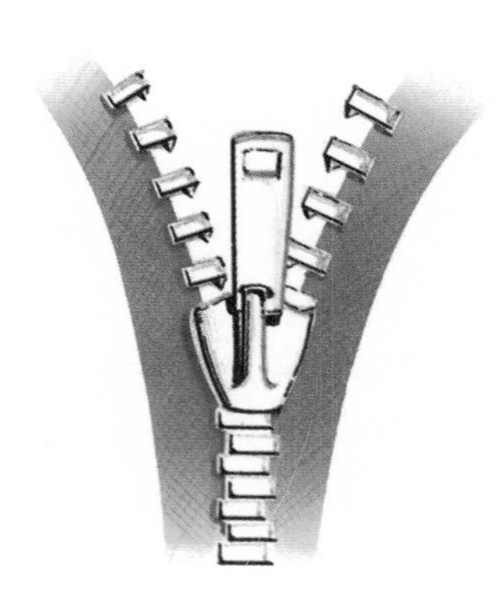

zip a fastener that joins two pieces of material together. **Zips** have teeth and a sliding catch.

zebra a wild animal like a horse with black and white stripes.

zebra crossing a part of the road marked with black and white stripes where people can cross safely.

zero nought. **Zero** is often written as 0.

zigzag going from left to right and back again.

zither a musical instrument that is played by plucking the strings.

zodiac the twelve birth signs used in the study of the stars. Aries and Gemini are two signs of the **zodiac.**

zombie a dead body that some people believe can be made to move by magic.

zone a region of a town or of a country.

zoo a place where wild animals are kept for people to come and see them.

Numbers

0	zero or nought	27	twenty-seven
1	one	28	twenty-eight
2	two	29	twenty-nine
3	three	30	thirty
4	four	40	forty
5	five	50	fifty
6	six	60	sixty
7	seven	70	seventy
8	eight	80	eighty
9	nine	90	ninety
10	ten	100	one hundred
11	eleven	199	one hundred and ninety-nine
12	twelve	200	two hundred
13	thirteen	300	three hundred
14	fourteen	400	four hundred
15	fifteen	500	five hundred
16	sixteen	600	six hundred
17	seventeen	700	seven hundred
18	eighteen	800	eight hundred
19	nineteen	900	nine hundred
20	twenty	1,000	one thousand
21	twenty-one	10,000	ten thousand
22	twenty-two	100,000	one hundred thousand
23	twenty-three	999,999	nine hundred and ninety-nine thousand, nine hundred and ninety-nine
24	twenty-four		
25	twenty-five		
26	twenty-six	1,000,000	one million

Colours

red yellow orange green blue

pink purple brown white black

Shapes

square circle

triangle oblong cube

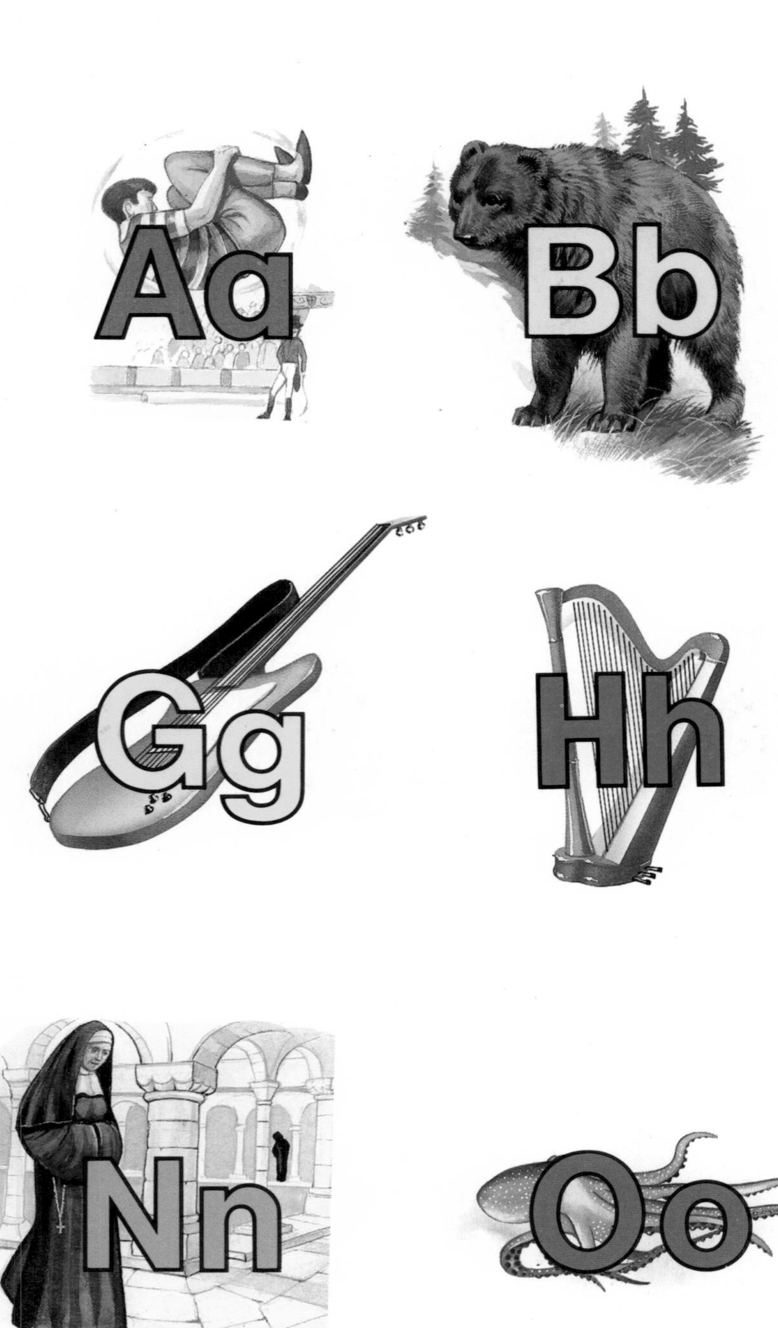
Aa
Bb
Gg
Hh

Cc

Ii
Jj

Nn

Oo

Pp

Uu

Vv

Ww